THE JOURNEY
TO EXCELLENCE

THE JOURNEY TO EXCELLENCE

MIKE ROBSON

M.R.A. INTERNATIONAL LTD.
WANTAGE, ENGLAND

Library of Congress Cataloging-in-Publication Data:

Robson, Mike.
   The journey to excellence.
   1. Organizational effectiveness. I. Title.
HD58.9.R62 1986   658.4   86-4044
ISBN 0 9513919 0 9

British Library Cataloguing in Publication Data:

Robson, Mike
   The journey to excellence.
   1. Quality circles
   I. Title
   658.4   HD66

ISBN 0 9513919 0 9

Printed and bound in Great Britain by
Wessex Press (Wantage) Ltd., England

CONTENTS

FOREWORD

Over the past few years thousands of people have spoken and written millions of words on the subjects of Quality and of Excellence. Most of the words have aimed at encouraging organizations to improve Quality and to become Excellent. Very few of the words, however, have told organizations how to go about it. The words have sparked off the imagination of people in many organizations and have stimulated the introduction of Quality and Excellence programmes of many shapes and sizes. Unfortunately the absence of a full-scale understandable and practical model has caused the demise of many such efforts. Some companies have merely attempted to implant Japanese systems into, often unwilling, Western organizations. The implants have usually been rejected, quite properly and understandably it should be said. Just as in medicine transplants will almost certainly be rejected without the most careful preparation of the receiving body, or if there is an intrinsic incompatibility between donor and recipient.

Other programmes have been introduced piecemeal, in no real order, and with no apparent or clear goal other than the vague intent of 'being Excellent'. These programmes are wish-fantasies, stand no chance of success, and every chance of giving a 'bad press' to a noble objective and eminently realizable dream, that of developing an organization which consistently meets the requirements of its customers, as it progresses in an orderly fashion along the road to the provision of defect-free goods and services.

What is required to make this possible is a model which is simple enough to be used by organizations in the real world, realistic enough to recognize that the whole organization must be drawn into the process, sensitive enough to isolate the requirements for change and provide the mechanisms for improvement, interesting enough to motivate employees, at all levels, to play their part, powerful enough to identify and continue to generate benefits for the organization and its people, and far reaching enough to become quite simply 'the way we do things around here'.

This is the model.

Part 1
THE FOUNDATIONS

Chapter 1

GROUND RULES AND BASIC REQUIREMENTS

This book has two objectives. The first is to interest people in the concept of Excellence and the second is to give a step by step practical guide which will assist organizations in structuring their 'Excellence programmes'. At the outset, however, we should perhaps note that the word 'programme' is probably a misnomer in this context, since programmes would generally be reckoned to have an end. To be more precise we are talking here about a process, something we buy into as a way of life, and work at constantly and consistently. With any other motivation or expectation, we will, quite simply, fail.

Excellence is not the preserve of any particular type of organization, neither is it a rigid, prescriptive and thus stultifying process. Excellent companies are actually not only more successful but also more fun to be in. Organizations such as IBM, Proctor and Gamble, Delta Airlines, Levi Strauss, MacDonalds, and Disney Productions are amongst those defined as 'Excellent' in a book published in 1982 and written by Peters and Waterman, called *In Search of Excellence*. The wide range of organizations on the list should give us all encouragement that it is possible for us as well. The commercial success of the organizations on the list should indicate that it is also worth while. The quest for Excellence is exciting and invigorating, just as its attainment is rewarding. Whether the organization is involved in high technology, consumer products, making hamburgers, or for that matter is a public utility, does not matter. Excellence is within the grasp of any organization.

Of course it is not easy, in fact quite the opposite, but looking at Excellent companies and assisting others in their struggle to become so, it is striking that there is no requirement for magic. As with most things in life success boils down to 98 per cent perspiration and 2 per cent inspiration!

There are, of course, a few utterly essential ground rules without which, frankly, it is not worth starting. By far the most important of these is the commitment of top management. Unfortunately in the last few years this has become a rather overworked phrase, so much so that it seems to have lost much of its meaning, and so it is necessary to specify what we mean by it and why it is so important.

A reality of organizational life, whether we like it or not, is that 80 per cent of what happens comes about as a direct result of management action. It is, therefore, absurd to think that the process of introducing and maintaining any significant change in an organization can be achieved without the active desire, cooperation and involvement of management, and specifically, since they establish policy, of top management.

In the past decade or so, some organizations have tried to escape this reality by introducing various 'bottom-up' mechanisms as a substitute. Let us say immediately that there is nothing wrong with 'bottom-up' mechanisms and concepts—they have a very important part to play in any process of achieving excellence—it is just that they cannot be a substitute. As someone once said, 'flowers grow from below but must be watered from above'. What, then, does management commitment mean and imply? Firstly, it involves being crystal clear about what it is we are trying to achieve on this 'Journey to Excellence'. Having clear goals will not only assist the top management concerned, but will be invaluable for all employees as they play their part in the process. Having this degree of clarity will help with the second requirement, which is that the top management group put all of their effort into winning the battle to achieve Excellence, rather than avoiding losing it by always playing safe. It is all too easy to lose the sharp edge that comes from focusing entirely on winning. The easy decisions on many occasions will be compromises which undermine the foundations of the process in the eyes of staff at all levels. It is therefore essential that we are able to avoid such situations.

An example of how easy it is to fall into these traps occurred in one organization concerning the appointment of the quality manager who would be responsible for the Excellence process. The chief executive had problems with several of his senior managers and initially was very tempted to push one of these 'problems' into the job. The person concerned would have been competent, if lacking in sparkle and flair. In the end, however, the person who was given the job was one of the best managers in the organization. It was fascinating to hear, over the ensuing few months, how people at all levels in the company had been watching for who would be appointed to this job.

As one person said, 'It was a clear indicator of the importance of the whole concept in the eyes of the top, rather like putting a poster on public display saying either "This is important" or "This is another game we're playing". The appointment told us it was for real!' It would have been so easy for the chief executive to have lost the winning edge by taking second best. If he had done so the whole process in that organization would have been negatively affected, if not destroyed.

The requirement for such decisions happens frequently and the third dimension of management commitment is the ability to stay 'on the tightrope'. The Journey to Excellence passes over some very difficult ground and there is a considerable requirement for what we could call 'tightrope ability'. This will help others in the organization to have confidence in the commitment being shown not only in the short term but over an extended period of time. All the experts in this field talk about years rather than months being needed to make significant progress, and some talk in terms of decades. Fortunately, however, although the journey has no end, there are enough milestones along the way to show us that we are making significant progress. Another aspect of this dimension, therefore, is the ability to maintain commitment, interest, and enthusiasm in the long run despite all the competing priorities which will be trying to draw us away from this focus.

Fourthly, top management needs to be able to communicate its commitment to the organization. This is another ongoing requirement. It is not enough merely to state our commitment to Excellence at the start and then to forget it. Equally it is not much good if we only ever tell ourselves in the mirror or the few people that we come into contact with regularly. Of course, different people and different levels require different kinds of communication and different frequencies of reinforcement. As a generalization, however, err on the side of too much, and try to communicate in practicalities and word pictures, rather than in theoretical abstractions.

Fifthly, top management need to do as they would have others do. Sometimes known as role modelling, this is an essential aspect of the day to day behaviour which is required. So often peoples' behaviour contains the hidden message 'do as I say, not as I do!'. When it comes to achieving Excellence, this cannot and will not work. The top management have to be the prime movers and they also have to be the arch exponents of the behaviour which will lead us all along the road to Excellence. It is no good simply telling our middle managers to communicate well, to develop their staff, to have clear goals, to plan, and so on, if we do not do the same. It is essential that top managers get out of their offices, go out, meet employees regularly, tell them directly of the real commitment that there is, sell the concept, recognize success. Schedule such 'walkabouts' into the diary well into the future and make them immoveable. When the top do it, middle managers and supervisors will find it much easier to do the same.

Overall, then, there is a need for the top not only to be committed, but to display that commitment, now and in the future. It is a requirement imposed by the rest of the employees of the organization and we must not let them down in this. Finally, there is also the need for faith: faith in the model which will take us on the journey, faith in our ability to lead the process, and faith in our people, for it is through them, ultimately, that Excellence comes to pass.

Chapter 2

PHILOSOPHY: 'THE WAY WE WANT TO DO THINGS'

Thomas Watson Junior, son of the founder of IBM and a one-time Chief Executive Officer of the Corporation wrote a book called *A Business and Its Beliefs*. In it he explains the beliefs upon which IBM is based. He says,

> IBM's philosophy is largely contained in three simple beliefs.
> I want to begin with what I think is the most important: our respect for the individual. This is a simple concept, but in IBM it occupies a major portion of management time. We devote more effort to it than anything else.
> Years ago we ran an ad that said simply and in bold type, 'IBM Means Service'. I have often thought it our very best ad. It stated clearly just exactly what we stand for. It also is a succinct expression of our second basic corporate belief. We want to give the best customer service of any company in the world.
> The third IBM belief is really the force that makes the other two effective. We believe that an organization should pursue all tasks with the idea that they can be accomplished in a superior fashion. IBM expects and demands superior performance from its people in whatever they do.

An utterly essential part of any process aiming at Excellence is that a philosophy is established for the organization in question. An even more important part is that it is adhered to. Even more important still is that it is believed by employees at large, for it is through them that Excellence comes to pass.

Why is a philosophy important?

The average employee in the average business has little or no idea about what his organization stands for and represents. Many do not even know what the company makes or sells, and even more do not fully understand. Before anyone laughs at such

6

outrageous notions he should carefully consider the situation in his own organization. To start with, is there an organized procedure for explaining to new employees what the organization is and what is its philosophy? Remember that here we are not asking whether or not there is some kind of induction procedure, we are asking specifically whether people are told what the organization stands for. It is a bizarre fact that very few organizations even know themselves what they stand for, and even fewer actually make a point of explaining it to their employees. If you believe that you do this in your organization it will be well worth checking how effectively the message has been received. Go out and ask ten people at random from different parts and levels of the organization to describe what it stands for.

At this point we need to establish that we are not here talking about our business objectives. In discussing the philosophy of an organization we are talking about something different. In a nutshell the goals are what we are trying to achieve whereas the philosophy gives us very fundamental guidance about how we are going to achieve them. This guidance is very much needed in a world full of options, confusions, and differing perceptions, which is why the philosophy of an organization is so important to everyone in the organization.

The reason for having a stated philosophy, value system, code of behaviour, call it what you will, is not to add a fancy, theoretical, and useless dimension to an already difficult process. Actually it is there to help, by giving clear and explicit guidelines for behaviour. If an action violates the philosophy then simply it is an inappropriate action within that organization. Starting at the top, senior managers need this guidance to help them direct the organization, since many of the choices that they have available are less than clear in today's world. Watson had something to say about this in *A Business and Its Beliefs*. It is worth repeating here.

> This then is my thesis: I firmly believe that any organization, in order to survive and achieve success, must have a sound set of beliefs on which it premises all its policies and actions. Next, I believe that the most important single factor in corporate success is faithful adherence to those beliefs. And finally, I believe that if an organization is to meet the challenges of a changing world, it must be prepared to change everything about itself except those beliefs as it moves through corporate life.
>
> In other words, the basic philosophy, spirit, and drive of an organization have far more to do with its relative achievements than do technological or economic resources, organizational structure, innovation, and timing. All these things weigh heavily in success. But they are, I think, transcended by how strongly the people in the organization believe in its basic precepts and how faithfully they carry them out.

Senior managers, then, need the philosophy to be clear and explicit because it is their job to advertise, promote, and disseminate it throughout the organization. Many of the difficulties of communication between the top and the rest of the business are caused by lack of the reference points we are talking about here.

For middle and junior managers the statement is essential as a guide and monitor of behaviour in the day to day struggle to achieve the goals of the department. The people 'in the middle' have a hard job in today's world, the pressures come from all around, and there are no easy answers. The philosophy helps because it guides behaviour by giving a backcloth against which judgements can be made. A manager might make wrong decisions but if he remains within the guidelines set he should not be far from the right spirit within his organization. Hopefully the philosophy will guide the process of deciding between various options, thus resulting in a higher quality of decision making.

In addition to management it is vital also to disseminate the philosophy to non-management staff. Many of the difficulties faced by companies stem from a lack of understanding about, or a positive lack of belief in, what the organization stands for. For an organization to stand any chance of becoming Excellent every employee must not only know the philosophy but must also believe it. This, of course, implies a considerable effort and investment for most companies. We need to get beyond fine words and gimmickry if we are to succeed here, and it is essential that we do.

What is a philosophy?

There are different ways of describing what is the philosophy of an organization. Sometimes it is known as the superordinate goal, alternatively the value system, the shared values, the philosophy, the code of ethics, or plain and simple, 'the way we do things around here'. The label does not matter too much. At root the philosophy expresses the core principles of the organization, and should give all employees clear guidance as to how to behave. It will be useful to look at some examples from different organizations. IBM's beliefs have already been mentioned but are worth repeating at this stage. They can be summarized as follows:

* Have respect for the individual.

* Achieve the best customer service of any organization.

* Do everything in a superior, and therefore excellent, manner.

This is an example of a useful and well-stated philosophy. It is clear, precise, and gives guidance as to how staff should behave and how managers should manage.

Of course different companies will have different statements since philosophies are not transferable. Another organization says, 'Our company is our customers and our staff.' Another draws a diagram to express its beliefs (Figure 1). At the Bank of America the philosophy is expressed as 'Leadership in serving people'. At Chubb Insurance they talk of 'Underwriting excellence'. Dupont say 'Progress through chemistry' and General Electric say 'Progress is our most important product'. Not all these examples will be equally effective in fulfilling the role of a superordinate goal.

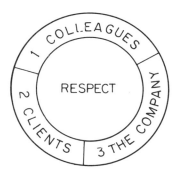

Figure 1

Indeed, although difficult to judge from the outside, some appear to be rather weak. To help us in working through ours, though, it will be useful to discuss in detail what we are trying to achieve in this statement, which is really designed to bind together all of the activities of the organization. Someone once said that it was the glue that held everything else together. One of its key functions is to give employees an unequivocal idea of what the chief exective would have done in whatever circumstances the staff find themselves. Having this will assist in standardizing behaviour throughout the organization and reducing inappropriate behaviour. This of course does not imply that employees will be conditioned to behave in one exactly standard way, since this would only serve to stultify individual expression, which in itself is an important aspect of Excellence. What it does mean is that everyone will have a guideline in framing their response to the issue at hand.

The second purpose of developing such a statement is an extension of the first, namely that it should provide guidance on the real priorities of the organization as far as the process of work is concerned. Again we are not here talking about the business goals of the organization, but the process of work, and the shared values statement should act as a tie-breaker in this respect, helping staff to decide between different ways of behaving.

Thirdly, the statement needs to reflect something about the expected values of employees whilst they are at work. Values are very deeply held in human beings and form the basis of what we consider to be right or wrong. The philosophy is well named when it is termed the 'shared values' statement in that it is deep and permanent, and expresses what the organization considers to be right.

Finally, the superordinate goal is designed to be, quite simply, an inspiration to employees, something to relate to and be proud of in their organization.

Of course it is difficult to assess with any degree of completeness the relative merits of different statements. Presumaby they are all felt to be worth while by the organization concerned, but it is likely that some will be more effective than others, and some of the examples given do not on the face of it appear likely to fulfil some of the requirements which have been listed. One or two stand out from the list already, given as extremely good ones, and these must certainly include IBM's. In three crisp statements, every employee of this wordwide organization is given clear instructions as to the expectations the corporation has of his behaviour.

Some people say that you can recognize an IBM employee from 50 paces because of the blue suit, or some other physical manifestation. In practice you often really can recognize someone from this distance, but it is more likely to be because he has this common behaviour base than that he wears a blue suit. This is the real uniform of the organization, and with a philosophy so strong and clear it is not surprising that the organization is the success that it is.

Since there are as many different philosophies as people, almost inevitably the value system will be generalized in nature, but certainly not to the point where it is bland and therefore useless. For example a shared values statement 'to be the best' is a grand and lofty idea but is not likely to be of much practical assistance to a line manager in the middle of a big operational problem with the production control system, or a member of staff with an irate customer on the end of the phone.

The statement is rather like a thumb print. It is an expression of the uniqueness of the organization and identifies it clearly and without fuss. But it is more than this. Our thumb prints have a lot of intricate detail on them, they are very precise, but that precision is not forced to our attention; it is there in the background whenever it is needed, it is a constant that we cannot rid ourselves of, it is the reference point of our individuality. So it is with the philosophy. We do not need or want a value system which cannot be expressed in less than 50,000 words, and yet it needs to contain a volume of beliefs. Platitudes in this whole area are worse than useless, rather like trying to distinguish the uniqueness of a person by saying that he has a head, rather than that he has a unique thumb print. This is why the philosophy of an organization is so extremely difficult to establish. It is an encapsulation of what the organization wants to be.

Often this will require back-up statements of explanation necessary to ensure that all staff understand the full meaning of the statement. A good example of this comes from a company in the medical field. BUPA Medical Centres Limited is an organization specializing in health assessment and education. The senior team of this organization met for two days and established their philosophy as:

To promote and maintain the good health and well-being of our individual customers and their enterprises through:

— recognizing and reaching agreement about their needs,
— care and professionalism in meeting those needs,
— long term commitment to this process.

This encapsulated their basic beliefs about the way they wanted to work as an organization. They then added definitions of some of the terms as follows:

Key definitions

Health
> The word health is used with its World Health Organization meaning, 'A state of complete physical, mental and social well-being, and not merely the absence of disease or infirmity'.

Individual
> The word individual here means one of us. Read as 'my'.

Customers
> Customers here include both our internal customers, who are the recipients of our individual work, and our external customers. These are the end users of our products and services, and include both individuals and corporate bodies, now and in the future.

Enterprises
> This word is used to include the sum total of the activities of the customer. In other words, if the customer comes to us as a private individual he and his family are the enterprise. Equally if he comes from an organization it includes the whole organization in all its facets. Because the word customer also applies to our internal customers the word enterprise for all of us applies in its internal sense to us, our families, and to BMCL.

Needs
> The word 'needs' applies to the aspirations and plans of those we deal with, as well as to their immediate requirements. It assumes that needs may change and therefore that they require constant attention.

Professionalism
> This word is used here to include the work done by all members of staff, not only those with professional qualifications. It implies meeting the needs of our customers to ever higher standards of performance. This in its turn means keeping up to date with new developments and opportunities in our own spheres, again, not only medically but in all areas of work.

Long Term
> This means for as long as we exist as an organization. It means that we are totally committed to this way of working.

This enabled them to brief every member of staff, not only about the statement itself but also in the wealth of meaning which underlies it. Ultimately people, of course, understand the whole meaning and do not need to refer to the 'dictionary', but at the outset it will often be an essential part of the process of establishing the philosophy since it will ensure that a full and complete understanding is passed over to all staff.

Setting the philosophy

There is no single right way of establishing the value system of an organization. Organizations which were founded by people of extraordinary vision are perhaps most fortunate. Hewlett and Packard, Wang, Disney, Strauss are all household names now, and their companies were built on the value systems they laid down. For these rare few the expression of the philosophy came from inside them as individuals. We do not know whether they thought it up whilst in the bath, had a burning mission in life, had a wild and crazy view of organizations that they were prepared to go bust for, or, as Martin Luther King, whether they had a dream. The two points that are essential for us are, firstly that they had an encapsulation of a way of doing things that they were prepared to commit themselves to absolutely, and secondly that they were able to express it in a clear and simple way which did not diminish the message, indeed which heightened it through making it possible for everyone to understand.

Most of us, however, are not in the process of founding a new business; we have the very difficult job of managing and working in companies which already have a history, organizations where employees have a vast series of expectations based on previous treatment, where managers often feel trapped within systems that they do not own, understand, or really believe in, where new ideas are greeted so often with a derisive 'in this place, you must be joking!'.

It is against this backcloth that we need to establish, communicate, and gain belief in our company's value system. To be honest, it is 50 per cent of the whole battle, and accordingly it is an extremely difficult process, not so much in the techniques used in defining it but certainly in the process of communication and even more so in the battle to gain belief and commitment to the statement from all staff at all levels. It also takes a long time, maybe years, though this will not stop the rest of the process from moving ahead.

The method for establishing the philosophy begins with the decision about who is to be involved in the initial part of the process. The answer, in one sense, is simple since it should be the 'owners' of the business. This, however, is not always easy to determine. What about subsidiary companies in a group? What about the trade unions? What about key 'opinion leaders'? There is no one right answer here, but the question raises an important point. At this stage we are trying to set shared values and since there is a danger that the chief executive of an ongoing business only gets to hear what others think he wants to hear, he should certainly consult with others, probably including an outside third party before the decision is made as to who should contribute to this vital first stage. Some guidelines which are designed to help this choice are, firstly, that in a private company the whole of the board of directors should be included. In a subsidiary company, meetings should be held within the governing board prior to deciding, to establish the importance of this stage and the genuine level of autonomy which is being afforded. Depending on the decisions made at this meeting, people from the governing board may or may not be needed in the group which is set up to establish this philosophy. In a family run business all of the members of the family who are involved in the organization need to be included. In a public utility it should be the senior group, again having had prior meetings with the next levels of seniority to establish the real extent of autonomy.

As well as the directors of the organization many organizations may wish to include key opinion leaders from amongst the senior management team and also the trade unions at this stage. The role of the unions will, of course, be crucial in the acceptance and dissemination of the value system when it is set, and however difficult and intractable the industrial relations problems may seem to be at the moment, it is worth bearing this in mind, and including key union officials from the start. Not only do they have an important role in disseminating the philosophy, they can be and very often are an essential part in its development.

Quite apart from their involvement and commitment to the journey there is also a benefit to be gained from drawing what are traditionally the 'two sides' of the organization together from the start and working together on the development of the value system, since this is a good way of beginning to develop a more productive 'win/win' philosophy to replace the normal 'win/lose' one.

Other points to be made about who should be involved are that, as far as possible, those who work on setting the statement should be around to introduce and disseminate it. It is not normally wise therefore to include in the group people who are on the point of retiring or those of such high mobility that they are not likely to be at the location for more than a few months.

Consultants, either internal or external, usually have an important role to play at a number of stages of this whole process, and this is one of them. Because they are disinterested parties they can help to force confrontation of the key issues and ensure that no false consensus is accepted. Both of these are, of course, essential if the result is to be worth while. Confrontation is a key part of the process of setting the philosophy, though this is not meant in the normally accepted sense of negative win/lose. If the process is to end with a philosophy worth disseminating there is a serious need to cut through easy platitudes and to get to core issues. It is the role of the consultant to set the structure which will facilitate this, and to work with the group to make sure that it happens in practice.

The timing of these meetings is, of necessity, imprecise, unlike the end product. It is not possible to predict how long it will take in any accurate way, though it is unlikely to take less than a day, and could take substantially longer.

The process of working on the philosophy itself falls into six main stages which are outlined below.

Step 1

Step one is to define the requirement for a philosophy in clear and precise terms and to gain a general understanding and acceptance of the need. A part of this phase will be to explain the role of the philosophy within the future workings of the organization. This is really essential for obvious reasons and a lot of work will probably have been done in the build-up to the first meeting to start this process.

Step 2

The next stage is to brainstorm the dimensions of the issue. To do this it will virtually always be essential to learn, or to relearn, the rules and procedures of brainstorming. Most groups are not good at creative thinking and since this may well give us the insights we need to set the right value system it is essential that this is done well. The brainstorming session would concern itself with the question: 'What are all the things we want this organization to stand for?' This session should be short and 'explosive', probably lasting no more than twenty minutes, and should be run by the consultant rather, for example, than by the chief executive, since it is essential to get all of the ideas of all the participating groups included at this stage.

Step 3

After the brainstorming meeting the meeting should be closed and members sent away to incubate the ideas. This might be for a rather extended lunch break, for a day or a week. For the longer periods of incubation it will be useful to have the list typed and give to members a copy so that they can refer to it during this period. The idea here is that rather than coming to a hasty, and maybe ill-considered, conclusion, that it will be better to spend some time mulling over the possibilities and letting them seep into our heads. So the incubation period can be of any length from an hour or so up to about a week, and it is important to build one into the structure and to insist on it before moving to the next stage.

Step 4

This stage involves the group in working towards establishing a statement. The brainstorming list can be a useful trigger for starting this discussion. This is the step which is likely to take a considerable amount of time as the different issues and nuances are weighed, and the desired nature of the business is explored from different perspectives. Again the presence of a third party is usually desirable here, since the debate needs to explore every relevant issue however difficult it might be to confront. A key point about the stage is that it is all too easy to come to a false consensus. Very often groups will claim to have come to an agreement very quickly, but usually when this is the case it transpires that not everyone is genuinely and fully committed to the statement and the consequences of it. It is essential here to remind people that this is not a paper exercise. We are saying that the day to day behaviour of everyone in the organization will be affected by the philosophy as it is ultimately stated and agreed at this meeting. It is a very serious issue by any token.

Many groups will allocate a full day or even two to this stage, and it is very unlikely that anything worth while will emerge in less than half a day. Whoever is running the session has a key role to play in encouraging people to keep ideas flowing and to keep many possibilities open. One of the big problems which affects the effectiveness of many groups is that they try to come to their decisions too quickly. They evaluate and throw out potentially useful ideas before they have really considered what use they might be. Successful groups keep as many options as they can on the table for as long as possible, and this is the aim here. In running the session it is very important that real sharing of ideas takes place and so flip charts or whiteboards are important. Individual contributions and agreements reached by consensus should all be recorded and posted around the room since this gives people the opportunity of looking back and reviewing the subject matter. It is as if the collected wisdom of the group is being displayed round the room, and this is central to good group process since it will ensure that more of us can remember more of the contributions that have been made. Remember that the contributions we forget we cannot use any more, so they become useless.

Once a true consensus has been reached and the statement has been carefully worded, with any notes of explanation that are needed, every member of the group should take a copy.

Step 5

Once the group has come to a real agreement it will be sensible for everyone to walk away from the meeting to mull over the agreed statement, and to make entirely sure that it is right for the individuals and also the organization. Having done this the meeting should be reconvened and a check should be made that every member of the group is still clear and committed to the philosophy. If not, then the particular concern will have to be considered, and the group will need to listen very carefully to any new thinking which is injected at this stage. It is all too easy, after the high level of investment which has been put into the exercise, to reject any new ideas which are put forward at this late stage. Obviously, however, it is important that no such rejection does occur. Ultimately, the group must be prepared to 'go back to the drawing board' and start the process again if the difficulty becomes intractable. Furthermore, it has to do this whilst maintaining the win/win spirit. Nothing will be gained here from slipping into a negative or critical attitude with anyone who does dissent or propose a new idea.

The end result of this stage will be a fully formed value system which is ready to be disseminated within the organization.

Step 6

The statement of philosophy represents an important and permanent part of the organization and it is sometimes useful to encapsulate it in some symbolic or permanent way. This can involve having the statement sculptured in wood or metal, having it written, signed, framed, and displayed somewhere public and prominent. There are different ways of doing this and the precise methods used by different companies will vary considerably. Deciding which method to use is often treated as an exercise in creative thinking and some splendid ideas can emerge from this final stage.

The outcome of this step is usually a few simple words—words, however, which are vital on the Journey to Excellence; words which are effectively the cornerstone of the edifice which we are in the process of building; words which tell every employee what is required as far as attitude and behaviour is concerned of everyone in the organization.

Chapter 3

CORE MISSION: 'WHAT WE ARE HERE TO DO'

The goals of an organization are different from its philosophy. In a nutshell, one is what we are trying to achieve and the other is how we are trying to achieve it. Organizations are complex, of this there is no doubt, and most do not respond well to this complexity. Confusion so often reigns. Ask the staff! Much of the problem of confusion relates to the subject of goals, and at the outset we should establish that there is no magic formula for avoiding it. We can, however, identify some of the key difficulties and propose mechanisms for working through the relevant issues.

The first difficulty associated with the goals of an organization is that there are different interest groups which put pressure on the organization to define the goals in a manner which favours their particular concern. For example, shareholders may be primarily interested in the immediate profitability of the organization, or possibly in ensuring its survival, whereas employees through their trade unions may be more concerned with short-term gain for themselves than anything else, and could even see high retained profitability in a definitely negative light. Some of the difficulties of setting short-term business goals for the next year relate to the constantly shifting balance of influence and power of these various interest groups. Almost inevitably there has to be give and take in the setting of such objectives, and it could be argued that if any one segment 'wins' too often or too much, then it is buying a longer term problem for itself since, as the balance of power tips the other way, the other groups will usually exact an appropriate revenge. This is one of the particular problems associated with politics becoming entrammelled in the business process, especially when the politics veers significantly either to the left or to the right. In practice what happens all too often is that a series of short-term victories by one side or the other are hailed with glee by the apparent winners whilst the losers lick their wounds and plot revenge. The victories are always pyrrhic if we look at the functioning of the organization in anything but the immediate term. Myopia is an all too common ailment of management and unions alike.

The second difficulty that organizations have with goals is that even if they can avoid the worse excesses of the first problem, they fall directly into the trap of inter-departmental goal conflict. Most organisations are structured in functions which therefore specialize in only one part of the business process. This all too often breeds insularity. The sales force wants to maximize sales revenue and needs high quality products to retain its customer base. Production is concerned with quotas pure and simple, whatever the quality. Warehousing is interested only in stock control, while the accountant's sole obsession is with whether or not his figures balance, and so on. Each function has its own specialized objectives and tries to maximize its perfor-mance. It all sounds perfectly sensible until it is realized that maximizing performance in one field often automatically limits the ability of another to do the same. Thus we get the classic finger-pointing arguments which occur in the vast majority of organizations. In most there is no organized method for getting out of this trap, and this leads to political games being played between departments, win/lose tactics, interpersonal strife, and so on, all of which in their turn contribute to making it all even worse.

The third difficulty concerns a phenomenon called goal displacement. Organiza-tions tend to be divided into functions and are structured hierarchically. This is the traditional way of trying to manage the complexities of dealing with numbers of people undertaking different tasks. As the organization becomes bigger and more complex, there is an increasing need for downward delegation of authority and respon-sibility within the functions. Organizations often have sophisticated mechanisms for defining the levels of such delegated authorities. Again, it all sounds very logical and sensible, but unfortunately the people in the process are not always either entirely logical or completely sensible. What so often happens is that people, sometimes because the organization imprisons its people within a rigid and stultifying bureau-cratic process, begin to regard the working of their function as an end in its own right. Stepping back from the situation it is easy to see that the work of any one function department or section is a partial means to achieve the overall end, which is what the organization is trying to achieve. Looking at it as many people do from within their own section, what they are doing becomes the end itself. Thus, for example, people apply the prescriptive bureaucratic rules to the absolute letter, and in so doing often negate the whole purpose of the organization. This is sometimes brought into sharp and painful focus with the workings of some of the departments which are supposedly employed to look after the welfare of the underpriveleged. Many of the well-reported tragedies affecting children, the elderly, the mentally ill, and so on, are, at root, to do with a blind adherence to the rules regardless of the obvious requirement of the afflicted and the equally obvious common-sense answer if the supposed objectives of the agency are to be achieved. The victim dies, the department holds an enquiry, the employee concerned says, 'I was just doing my job.' Examples including such human tragedy are, of course, more vivid than others, but the fact that such situations exist in most organizations of any size is equally tragic. Neither can we fob off the phenomenon with an accusation that the staff concerned behaved pathetically. It is by no means as easy as that. Often, indeed usually, the organization is culpable. When, to take a recent simple example, a traffic warden gives parking tickets to a hearse and mourners' cars we cannot end our analysis of the situation necessarily with a statement about the warden's insensitivity and stupidity in such situations; we often also have to consider that the·organization told him to do a job, bound him in red tape and gave him no degree of freedom within which to adjust his behaviour appropriately.

Another variation on goal displacement which often occurs happens when the original objectives of the organization get lost as people focus their attention on maintaining the organization as it is and therefore their own place in the power structure. An example of this was quoted by Robert Michels in his book *Political Parties* where he highlighted the fact that the leaders of some socialist and labour organizations in Europe, once they had achieved a position of power, spent their time seeking to maintain this, thus subverting the original democratic aims of the organization. He calls this process 'The Iron Law of Oligarchy', and certainly looking around organizations in both private and public sectors there is clear evidence that many of them do operate self-perpetuating oligarchies—a reality which often takes them far away from the original purpose of the organization as defined.

These three difficulties are faced to a greater or lesser degree by most organizations, and one of the main reasons why so many find it so difficult to overcome them is that they have no core mission to fall back on and refer to. The core mission of an organization defines in a simple communicable way what is the fundamental purpose of the organization. In most organizations most of the staff do not know this. Amazing though it may sound it is so, and please let us not separate our own company from this. It is all too easy to assume that everyone must know, without realizing how difficult it is to achieve and how few organizations have staff in them who are fully clear why they are doing what they are doing.

The core mission, in defining clearly and precisely what we are trying to achieve in the organization, fulfils the very useful function of being a 'tie-breaker'. If any manager or member of staff is torn between two actions, referring back to the core mission should assist in the making of the decision. As such the core mission statement has to communicate a clear and precise message. It needs to be short and succinct but to encapsulate what the organization is really trying to achieve. There is a trap here that many organizations fall into, which is to define the mission in broad and often ambiguous terms designed to justify the existence of the institution. Such statements are not only useless as 'tie-breakers' but they often also belie the actual

19

operational goals that people pursue in the organization. Thus, for example, a mental institution may have as its official goal 'the treatment of mental illness', whereas the actual goal being worked on by the staff might be much more to do with the custodial care of the inmates and have very little to do with treatment of their illness. The core mission is not designed to be a bland, politically acceptable statement; it must be precise and accurate since it will be used in a day to day sense by people all over the organization to help them make difficult decisions.

Setting the core mission of the organization will be the first agenda item at a meeting, or series of meetings. Having done this the next step is to define the key factors that will be essential in achieving it.

It is unlikely that the core mission of an organization of any size will be set in less than one or two days. This is not meant to imply that people do not know what they are doing at the moment, merely that there is a real requirement for absolute clarity when it comes to the fundamental goals of the organization. So often the reality is that people actually do their job without any real understanding of the framework within which it is set. How many times after he has done something 'wrong', and when the context is finally explained, does an employee say, 'Why didn't you tell me, if I'd known I wouldn't have done that!'

Any Excellence process has to recognize the need for the contribution of the people, since without it the process simply will not work. For this to be used successfully everyone needs to know, fundamentally, what the organization is trying to achieve. Most organizations also fail fully to recognize the need within people for a structure and clearly defined framework within which to work. The majority of companies actually induce people to work as a part of a process without letting them know what the end product is, let alone what the organization is trying to achieve. Look at it from the point of view of the new employee. The first day in a new job and what do we often get? We may get a skimpy induction programme which does little to answer our real needs, and then we are put to work, which is fine because that is what we came for, but so often nothing else, maybe for ten years!

Any Excellence process needs to motivate and encourage the employees, since without them there is no progress, and this is no way to motivate the employee.

The process of setting the core mission or basic objective of the business involves getting together the same core group that set the philosophy unless there are particular reasons for changing it. This stage of the process will also probably require the attendance of an outside party, who may be either an internal or external consultant to assist in ensuring a focus on the real issues. It is very easy to slip off the central purpose in sessions such as these and to end up dealing with peripherals and trivialities. It has already been said that it is unlikely that the setting of the core mission will be accomplished in less than one or two days and so at least this amount of consecutive time should be set aside. Many organizations use a weekend to work on this issue. Though this is not essential, an important practical point is that if the meeting is fragmented it will definitely take longer, so in the interests of economy, efficiency, and effectiveness it will be as well to try to work the main part of the issue through in one go.

The agenda at the meeting is simple to define and difficult to achieve. The goal is to state and agree the core mission, or fundamental purpose of the business, and to do so in terms that are both practicable and useful for all employees. At the outset there will usually be a requirement for the third party consultant to outline the need for such a statement and the process whereby we will work on this issue. After this there is often a period of difficult and embarrassed silence! It is actually remarkably difficult to work out, agree, and state what a business is really trying to achieve above all else. This is so even in many husband and wife teams, let alone corporations of any size.

What will usually happen at this stage, after the embarrassed silence, is that everyone will very quickly come to an agreement that the fundamental purpose of the organization is 'to maximize its profit' or some other generalized statements of the same nature. This actually is neither useful nor true for the vast majority of companies. If maximizing profit were the only objective then most organizations are in the wrong business. If they insist, then suggest the fields of sex and drugs as being more lucrative! Even within their fields there are few institutions that really wish to pursue profit regardless of anything else as their goal, and even where they do, they need to answer questions of the time scale—is it profit in the short, medium, or long term—and also what is meant by this and how it is going to be regulated and defined.

This is not meant to imply that profit is unimportant; obviously it is. In practice, however, it is far more likely that the core mission of the company will be defined in rather different and probably more useful terms. It is important to recognize that this statement is not a hollow shell; it is there for a very real purpose. If everyone is not clear where we are trying to go as an organization, then it is very unlikely that we are going to get there, and certainly we will not be working as a team as we try. This is why it usually takes so long to work through the issues, because everyone who takes part brings with him his own set of perceptions, standards, and ideas. We often tend to assume that everyone else thinks and feels the same way as us and there is the beginning of the problem.

It is because of this that the process is so important. Magnetism provides a graphic analogy of what we are trying to do. Most organizations contain people who, in terms of goals, are all pointing in different directions, rather like iron filings tipped onto a table at random, the differing directions relating both to their perception of their organization and also, of course, to their private lives. We all know that people do think, see, feel, and behave in remarkably different ways, and what we are trying to do in setting the core mission is to give a common focus so that the 'iron filings' can gain strength (magnetism) through aiming in the same direction. It is remarkable how much organizational strength is dissipated in most companies because people assume that it is obvious what the organization is trying to achieve, whereas in practice there is no common focus, indeed there are often people who are actively pulling in different directions. We only need to look to the fruitless win/lose battles that go on between departments, individuals, unions, management, and so on, to give a clear indication of the point being made. Sometimes it appears that we are trying to assist our business competitors rather than defeat them!

The process of setting the core mission then is not easy. Having overcome the embarrassed silence and the false consensus the discussion is likely to be lively if the meeting is run well! It is remarkable how many different views there can be about what we are really trying to achieve, and it is because of this that it is so important to work the issue through successfully. At this stage of the proceedings it is important to keep the issues alive for as long as possible and not to arrive at a conclusion too quickly.

In the West we have an unfortunate tendency to come to premature conclusions that we regret later. It is very important that this does not happen in this debate because we are committing ourselves to objectives that will determine our future. There is a striking analogy which indicates the difference between the East and the West. It concerns how we teach our soldiers to shoot. In the East it is said they line up their new recruits with a rifle and give instructions:

Ready ready ready ready,
Aim aim aim aim,
Fire!

In the West the system is the same but the instructions are different.

Ready,
Fire!
Aim

In this work we should be careful not to fall into the trap of coming to a view too quickly since real consensus does take time to achieve and we must avoid a false consensus. It is no good appearing to agree or reaching a soft compromise on this issue. Nothing short of a full-blown consensus will suffice, and everyone must be prepared to nail their colours to the mast when the decision is reached.

Because of this there is a requirement for the meeting to be run in a particular way. Basically, in running the meeting the technique must be one of constantly throwing the suggestion back into the court and keeping the list of possibilities open for as long as possible, rather than trying to force any suggestion into a possibly false agreement. The agreement will come when it is right and there should be no pressure to get at it sooner by whoever is running the meeting. Clearly, managing this process requires a considerable amount of skill, and this should be borne in mind when planning the event.

Having established the core mission there is a further need; this is to determine what the key factors will be in achieving success with it. These are the 'cold sweat' factors, those without which the mission cannot be accomplished. Thinking through these elements and defining them in appropriate action sentences will be important ultimately to the whole goal-setting process in the organization, since it will focus attention on the truly key items. The task of agreeing the key success factors and then of assessing current performance in achieving them will often be the job of the full group that defines the core mission. There will be circumstances, however, in which it will make more sense to establish a smaller group to think this aspect through. Either way, in most cases this whole subject will be tackled at a separate meeting.

Part 2

BASICS— THE SCAFFOLDING

It is no good fantasizing that Excellence can be produced out of mid-air. It requires the foundations which are provided by the philosophy and the core mission statements, and it has to be built within a framework which will allow it to stand solid. Developing this framework is the next stage of the journey.

In practice there are six major areas that require attention and these are dealt with in this part of the book. The fact that these are basic features, well known as being fundamental to organizational success, should not lead anyone either to assume that they are self-evident or that the issues have been sufficiently dealt with already in their organization. Many of the obstacles to Excellence in most companies can be removed by getting right the issues dealt with in this section.

The chapters in this part of the book are arranged first to explore the issue, by giving an outline of the key dimensions which are needed to ensure Excellence in the basic topic being discussed, and then to propose a process by which current performance can be audited.

The six major basics which must always be included are as follows:

* Organization structure
* Management competence
* Communications
* Customer orientation
* Ownership
* Trust

It is of course possible in some organizations that other basic considerations need to be added. This is perfectly in order and they should be added to the original six. The remaining chapters in the part take us through these issues in turn.

Chapter 4

ORGANIZATIONAL STRUCTURE

Organization structure

One of the most powerful determinants of what happens in an organization is its structure. Although some would have it otherwise, it is not actually the ultimate influence, but it is inarguably very significant and has been for centuries. In a famous quote, Petronius Arbiter in 210 BC commented:

> We trained hard—but it seemed that every time we were beginning to form up into teams we would be reorganised .... We tend to meet any new situation by reorganizing, and a wonderful method it can be for creating the illusion of progress while producing confusion, inefficiency and demoralization.

Many companies go through spasms of reorganization, from decentralized to centralized, from pyramid to matrix, from functional to project. Many of these changes are both important and significant at certain stages of an organization's life, but they are not really fundamental in any general sense to the achievement of Excellence. There are, however, some generalizations about structure which are relevant to this discussion, the first of which concerns size.

In many companies and institutions, especially larger ones, employees feel estranged, alienated, separated from anything that is important to them: they feel that they are there 'just to do a job'. This causes vital problems both to the people and the organization. Whereas, however, the individual will certainly be able to rationalize his own behaviour to the detriment of the organization, the organization will be left with the inevitable economic reality associated with having demotivated staff, and also the social responsibility of having caused it.

As such, organizations striving for Excellence will be well advised to build their structures in a way that their people can relate to. This does not mean having entire organizations built of family-sized, autonomous groups, but what it does mean is that care over the likely human effects should be a key part of organization design. Stories are rife about large-scale, fully automated, futuristic organizations which have been plagued not only by strikes from a workforce that feels 'dehumanized' but also by actual sabotage. The original industrial saboteurs, the Luddites, felt threatened by the introduction of machinery. The present-day threat, that of being dehumanized, is felt to be even more insidious by many, and unless it is managed successfully, Excellence will not be achieved. Furthermore, with the rapid escalation of sophisticated computerized machinery across a wide range of industry, this problem will, in time, become increasingly significant.

In designing organizations, then, many of which will be large, it is necessary to build a framework that people can relate to easily and naturally, and that at least feels small. In small companies, pretty well whatever their structure and style, there is a noticeable shortening of lines of communication. People seem able to relate more easily to the aims of the organization, and seem to feel more able to gain access to senior people if they wish to.

The implication of all this for the large organization which is on the Journey to Excellence is to design the structure in fairly small 'profit' or 'accountability' centres. The appropriate size will clearly depend on the organization and the particular function, but up to three hundred people is a good number to aim at.

Organizations or units of up to three hundred people are substantial; they are, moreover, small enough for the senior person to remember everyone's name (if he has a bad memory he should go on a training programme to improve it, at least to this level!). Furthermore, a three hundred person unit, even within a big organization, is large enough to have its own clearly definable goals, strategies for achieving those goals, and also management style.

The second generalization continues with this same basic principle, that of building structures which allow people to relate, and concerns the issue of centralization or decentralization. There should be a tendency towards decentralized structures wherever possible. Centralized structures all too often focus inward on their own bureaucracy, rather than outward towards the ultimate customer. Ask customers everywhere how infuriating this is. We have all been in situations where people say, 'Sorry but the computer isn't set up that way' or 'Sorry, but that's not in our system'. Organization structures need to be flexible enough actively to help customers rather than frustrate them and it is often the structure itself which has an influence on this, as well as the attitudes and behaviour of the people in it.

A vivid example of the effects of decisions about centralizing and decentralizing concerns the recent history of the British Leyland Motor Company and specifically Jaguar Cars.

Once one of the great names in British car manufacture, Jaguar was swallowed up in that most sorry of 'centralizations' as British Leyland was created during the period when 'big' was popularly supposed to be 'beautiful'. The fall from grace was rapid. With nothing to relate to but a remote hierarchy located in an ivory tower somewhere else, pride disappeared and was substituted by increasingly poor quality and, surprise, surprise, a rapidly diminishing order book. Not until the late 1970s with the Michael Edwarde's regime was this folly reversed. Jaguar was given back its identity, pride began to be restored, quality improved, and drew along with it a progressive and then rapid improvement in sales. Of course, this did not happen by magic and neither was it as simple as this illustration appears to suggest, but it is important to understand that Jaguar would not have been 'turned round' without being given back its identity. The general point being made here is that small really is 'more beautiful' than big. Wherever there is a choice, choose the 'small' option and build a decentralized structure.

The third generalization is a natural extension of this second point and concerns the balance between staff and line roles. Big, centralized organizations often have massive staff sections, which generally speaking are most effective at frustrating and annoying the people in the line who do the productive work. Cruel, maybe, but all too often the case.

The 'ivory tower' syndrome is familiar to anyone who has worked in a large organization and can be immensely frustrating. Of course some staff functions have an important part to play in most organizations, but they should certainly be kept as small as possible. Furthermore, it is remarkable how often the work that is done as a staff function can be achieved more productively, effectively, and cheaply by giving the responsibility to the line. As such there should be a regular review of whether activities which are currently the responsibility of staff functions would be better transferred out to the line.

The fourth generalization recognizes that because staff and line roles are significantly different there is always likely to be a certain amount of misunderstanding. Equally, however, this can be minimized by making sure that people, as far as possible, do not get stuck in staff roles, and are rotated into line jobs at least every few years. In this way they do not get stale and can gain from the experience just as much as line personnel can benefit from periods in staff roles.

The general rules with regard to the line/staff balance are firstly that staff functions should be kept as small as possible, either by doing away with them or integrating the work into normal line responsibilities, and secondly that personnel should be rotated into and out of the remaining staff roles, thus avoiding, as far as possible, the danger of developing 'staff professionals' who, experience dictates, can so easily lose touch with reality.

The fifth generalization again links with the last point. Structures should be designed so that as many people as possible are as close to the end customer as possible.

Every employee in the organization has 'internal' customers, a concept that will be dealt with in detail in a later section of the book, but here we are talking about the end user of the goods or services we produce and sell. Keeping people in clear sight of this most important of animals is key in designing structures. The further away the customer appears to be, the less people will be able to relate to him and the more likely that shoddy work will be passed on uncorrected, whereas there are few people who would sell an obviously faulty item direct to the customer. It is a simple but vital recognition and one that is central to the whole concept of Excellence.

In summary, then, there are five generalizations that are useful regarding organization structure. They are:

* Keep the discrete units as small as possible.
* Decentralize rather than centralize.
* Keep staff sections as small as possible.
* Do not leave people in staff positions for too long.
* Keep people as close to the end user as possible.

If this is what we need to achieve, we next require a mechanism for auditing what we have at the moment. This information will be a mixture of factual analysis and opinions.

It will be important, of course, not simply to rationalize away the value of looking for improvements on the basis that what we have at the moment seems to be satisfactory; as such it will usually be a good idea to involve and audit team in this task, assisted and facilitated by the internal or external resources that are working with the process. Audit teams, which are the main mechanisms for looking at the basic issues affecting organizations, are small groups of employees, ranging in level from top to bottom depending on the topic. The groups are selected by management or the Excellence steering group and are given a precise brief with a budget of time which includes both length and frequency of meetings. They are helped in their work by a facilitator.

Generally speaking the composition of the audit team which works on this issue should be based round management. Clearly a key task of top management is to design structures appropriate to the type of organization and its stage of development, and so it will be sensible to involve senior people in this group. It may also, however, be a very useful idea to include two or three (not one) other people from different levels of management to introduce a different perspective and perhaps even to play a 'devil's advocate' role. If this is done it will be important to select people who will not be overawed and secondly who will not fall into the trap of only saying what they think the senior people want to hear. The total size of this group should not exceed seven.

The brief given to the group members should be to investigate and report, with recommendations, on the factors within the current organizational structure which would be likely to inhibit or promote the achievement of Excellence. The report should take the form of a management presentation in which all members of the group play a part, backed up by a short information pack covering the key items. It should be made absolutely clear that making observations and recommendations about individual managers is not a part of the brief and that they should steer well clear of this area. The broad structure that the group should be encouraged to follow is as follows:

Step 1.   Clarify mutual understanding of the brief. Agree group norms to be used in working together.

Step 2.   Having read this chapter, discuss its contents and come to a broad agreement about its appropriateness in relation to the organization in question. Record the details of the consensus.

Step 3.   Map the organization structure as it stands. This should not only include drawing a conventional organization structure but should also look at features which are less commonly evaluated. Gather samples of factual information, for example about the length of time people stay in staff positions, the amount of movement that takes place within the organization, the distances between people in a range of jobs and the end customer. This list is meant neither to be exhaustive nor mandatory but to give examples of possible areas of importance and interest.

Step 4.   Look at these data alongside the conclusions reached at step 2. Record details of this consensus. Make extensive use of the 'what if' question to explore, creatively, possible ways of solving problems which have been highlighted. Keep the issues open for a while; do not come to premature conclusions.

Step 5.   Highlight aspects of the current structure which are more likely to promote the achievement of Excellence. Record details of the consensus.

Step 6.   Form the details of any recommendations to cover items which are likely to inhibit Excellence. Play devil's advocate to check them out.

Step 7.   Prepare a management presentation backed up by a brief written report containing an outline of the work and facts on which the conclusions and recommendations have been based.

Step 8.   Give the management presentation and draw up an action plan based on the results of the discussion after the presentation.

Step 9.   Track progress in achieving action plan as agreed.

This group should be given a maximum of fourteen weeks to present its findings and the meetings should not, under normal circumstances, be more frequent than weekly and not last for more than one and a half hours. They should be scheduled ahead of time and in a 'same time, same place, next week' fashion. This avoids unnecessary work in coordinating diaries, meeting rooms, etc. Action minutes must be produced as a result of every meeting and circulated to interested parties.

Chapter 5

MANAGEMENT

Quality and Excellence can only be built on a foundation of good management principles and practice, of this there is no doubt. As such it is essential that no effort is spared in ensuring this in both the short and the long term.

Unfortunately many organizations buy themselves years of unsatisfactory performance through paying insufficient attention to the selection of supervisors and managers. It is worth remembering that over 80 per cent of the progress towards Excellence will come about as a direct result of competence amongst supervision and management, and that one mistake in selection will always attract a disproportionately high cost in terms of both the work being done in the department concerned and the people performing it.

In most organizations it will not immediately be possible to correct mistakes that have already been made, so the policy will need to be one of 'cure' in the short term and of 'prevention' for the longer run. There are three main aspects of this basic topic covering firstly the selection of managers and supervisors, secondly how they are helped to focus on areas that are priorities, through goal setting, appraisal, and counselling mechanisms, and thirdly how they are equipped for improving their performance in their current role, and also for future positions, through training and development to improve their knowledge and skills. All three aspects are vital and need to be looked at separately, possibly by up to three different audit teams.

Aspect 1—Selection

For the future it is essential to utilize a coherent set of criteria for selection which takes into account the requirement not only for specialist technical knowledge but also the ability in managing people. An undue emphasis on the technical ability required has so often led to one of the most common and fatal of all selection errors. This is especially prevalent at supervisory levels and involves the tendency to promote the most technically competent operator to the supervisory job. Unfortunately this person often has no aptitude for the managerial role and so the company ends up gaining a bad supervisor and losing a good operator. Management involves getting things done through other people and only people who have proven or likely skills in doing just this should be promoted to these jobs.

At more senior levels of the organization what is basically the same phenomenon is called 'The Peter Principle' after its originator, who declared that people in organizations tend to rise to the level of their incompetence!

To avoid these fatal traps it should be standard practice for all management and supervisory jobs to have not only a job description but also a person specification. The latter document should contain a description of the characteristics of the ideal candidate for each job. The description will be different for different jobs depending on such things as the technical nature of the work done in the department, the type of people to be managed, the likely style of management which will be appropriate at the outset, previous experience, age, and so on. As with the job description, which outlines the key areas of responsibility in the job and the main tasks to be fulfilled, the person specification needs to be a 'live' document which is updated regularly in the light of changing circumstances. To assist in the process of selection, appropriate use should be made of personality inventories, management style questionnaires, and other such instruments, as well as the conventional job interview. The use of such mechanisms is formalized in some companies in their use of so-called 'assessment centres' or 'career development centres'. Certainly these can be valuable, especially in medium and larger organizations where many of the candidates for supervisory and management jobs will be internal and there will be an ongoing need for a 'stockpile' of suitable candidates.

All of the foregoing implies that, if it exists at present, the 'dead man's shoes' method of selection has to be dispensed with. Such a policy clearly introduces fatal weaknesses into the management team and must be avoided at all costs. Of course it is all too easy to assume that it is only big public utilities that would ever dream of employing such apparently crazy methods, but there is in practice a good deal of it which is embedded into the systems of many companies. It is important to be rigorous in unearthing any such tendencies. It is difficult enough to achieve Excellence anyway, without having to play the game with a 'B' team.

This is an important enough issue to warrant investigation, again typically via an audit team. There is a danger here of course; this is that people who have been selected as managers or supervisors by the present system may be loath to criticize it lest it implies a criticism of their own competence. Many organizations are, in practice, self-perpetuating oligarchies, and they suffer from all the deficiencies, such as congenital weaknesses and exaggerated features, that in-breeding can give rise to. As such it will be important in the selection of members of this group to be aware of the danger and to make it a formal part of the briefing at the outset.

Clearly the personnel director has a role to play in the activity and should be invited to join. Apart from him, there are no absolute rules about the composition of the group other than that it would seem to be appropriate to restrict it to managers and supervisors since the topic concerns these levels of people.

It will often be appropriate to include people from different levels of management since this will broaden the perspective. The size of this group should be no more than five people. The brief for the work is to investigate the present system of selection for supervisory and management positions, and to recommend any improvements which will improve the calibre of the management and supervisory team in the short, medium, and long term. It should be made clear in the briefing that the group is not there to make comments on, or to appraise, the performance of any individual in the company.

The broad structure that the group should follow in its work is as follows:

Step 1.   Clarify mutual understanding of the brief and agree group norms to be used in the meetings.

Step 2.   Having read the relevant portion of this chapter, discuss its contents and come to an agreement about its relevance and importance in this organization. Add any other standards which are relevant and on which there is common agreement. Record details of the consensus.

Step 3.   Collect factual data about the processes currently in operation for recruitment and selection, remembering that they may be different for different levels and different functions.

Step 4.   Research potentially useful mechanisms such as assessment centres, personality inventories, and so on, as deemed appropriate for the organization in question.

Step 5.   Analyse the current methods using an analytical technique such as the six-word diagram. Draw conclusions from the analysis.

Step 6.   Form the details of any recommendations. Use the devil's advocate technique to ensure that they are capable of working in the 'real world'.

Step 7.   Prepare a management presentation and back-up report.

Step 8.   Give the presentation and draw up an action plan on the basis of the discussion after the presentation.

Step 9.   Track progress, making sure that actions agreed are completed on time.

This group should be allocated up to fourteen weeks to present its findings. Meetings should be held regularly and on about a weekly basis. It will be possible for the group to be working on different steps in the process simultaneously; for example steps 3 and 4. Meetings should be scheduled for about an hour, and never longer than two hours. Action minutes must be produced as a result of every meeting. As far as possible the meetings should be organized into a regular pattern to save time in diary planning.

Aspect 2—Goal setting, appraisal, and counselling

The second fundamental in ensuring that managers play their part in the process of achieving Excellence is to have an organized method for helping them to decide their priorities, and also assess their performance, with a view to improvement in the future. The requirement here is for a series of processes which all too often are introduced piecemeal, and therefore unsuccessfully, into organizations. They represent some of the basics of personnel management, however, and no Excellent company can afford to be without them. Do not be put off by stories of failure in introducing these mechanisms—they only fail if introduced out of context and with no clear aim in mind. The mechanisms being referred to are, firstly, job descriptions. If a manager is to be effective he needs to know what he is supposed to be responsible for doing—the key dimensions of his job. Often, and unfortunately, the personnel departments of organizations undertake the large-scale task of writing job descriptions, only to file them and let them gather dust. To be useful these must be made active documents to be used for reference and reminder purposes by the job holder and manager alike. They also need to be kept up to date. Jobs change, like everything else, and an out of date job description is neither helpful nor credible. The job description is then the basic document for helping to ensure that management know what they are being paid to do.

What is required now is a mechanism for setting short-term targets for managers to work towards in a few particularly key areas of their jobs. Mechanisms for this are called by many names, and were popularized in the 1960s under the banner of 'management by objectives'. The very words bring cynical smiles to the faces of vast numbers of managers, who have suffered the ill-effects of badly conceived and badly managed management by objectives programmes, which were literally paper-generating and time-eating machines, with no credibility in the eyes of the average line manager, whose only hope of avoiding being inundated was often to manipulate the system. Tragically memories of such programmes are still vivid, and yet management by objectives as a concept remains immensely powerful and utterly essential. It was the execution which was handled so badly, and we must learn the lessons from these experiences. We cannot avoid the requirement for managers to be working within the framework of a set of objectives that give both him and the organization a means of measuring success and ensuring that all the necessary key tasks are tackled.

The key in avoiding the problems of the past is to ensure that the activity is a line responsibility rather than something which line people perceive was dreamed up in what they see as being the ivory tower of the central personnel department.

The activity must be owned by the management team and so they must understand its role and importance. They do not want a further bureaucratic requirement imposed on them, and this aspect of the system should be kept as simple as possible. Progressively, and as the individual managers get used to the system, the objective setting should be done more and more by the manager himself, and then ratified and amended through discussion with his boss.

Thus far we have a system for ensuring that managers know what their main job responsibilities are and a mechanism for people to use to set their specific short-term targets, which look up to a year ahead and which relate to two or three of the key result areas for the next period of time.

The next step is a system for reviewing achievement, assisting the process of setting the next round of goals, and for helping to improve performance still further in the subsequent round. Typically the mechanism used here is an appraisal and counselling system. Again in many organizations this is viewed with rather bored disdain, protestations about the time it takes to fill the forms in, and an assertion that 'I talk to my people all the time anyway'. Do not be misled! Excellence is not possible without an organized mechanism for helping managers to quantify what they intend to achieve and for working on opportunities to improve performance. This is not to say that people are always inaccurate when they claim that their present system 'achieves nothing', that it is a 'form-filling exercise', and so on, merely that so often the real purpose behind the system has been swallowed up and lost in the process of implementation.

As far as appraisal and counselling systems are concerned, however, this is not the only problem. A further and very significant difficulty is that most managers are neither competent nor confident in running such meetings, and at the bottom of it all this causes many managers to feel a high level of anxiety which so often translates itself into negative comments about the mechanism itself. Training and practice in conducting these meetings is a key ingredient for success and should be backed up with 'on the job' development, involving help and assistance for people, in the first one or two years. One further point concerning appraisal and counselling is that it must operate from the very top of the organization. It is truly amazing how many systems are imposed on the middle and lower ranks of the organization, but when it comes to the question of the top being part of it the response is 'We talk to each other anyway!', 'Our jobs are different', 'It wouldn't work for us!', and so on. These are the same comments heard from everywhere else in the organization!

At this point it is perhaps appropriate to remind ourselves that Excellence requires that management, from top to bottom, behave in a way which is in line with what they expect others to do. 'Do as I say, not as I do' happens everywhere in organizations and needs to be eradicated if management is to be credible. If Excellence is to be achieved, 'do as you would be done to'.

This subject again requires an audit team to help assess the current status and recommend future developments which would put the company in good shape for achieving Excellence. This group should consist of a 'diagonal slice' of the management and supervision of the organization to ensure that views from all levels are represented. If it is felt appropriate that non-management staff be included in the goal setting, appraisal, and counselling system, even on a voluntary basis, then it will be wise to include one or two staff in the group as well. The group should contain no more than nine people, and should be smaller if possible. The brief for this group is to investigate the current systems for ensuring that managers and supervisors ('all employees', if everyone is to be included) have an organized method for deciding their priorities and assessing their performance with a view to improvement in the future. The group should be briefed to report on current systems and recommend improvements which are necessary to ensure that the performance of management can be developed to a level which could genuinely be described as excellent.

It is recommended that the group works within the following broad structure:

Step 1. Clarify mutual understanding of the brief and agree norms to be used during group meetings.

Step 2. Having read the relevant portion of this chapter, come to a view about its relevance and importance in this organization. Record details of the consensus.

Step 3. Collect data about the different aspects of the current situation. It may be useful to think in terms of designing a short questionnaire to elicit a wider range of views from across the organization to help answer such questions as

(a) the perceived usefulness of current job descriptions,

(b) whether there is a formal procedure for setting objectives,

(c) whether the goal-setting process is seen as being overly bureaucratic,

(d) whether people perceive that there is an organized appraisal and counselling system (it is amazing how often there is a scheme supposedly in use and yet people perceive that they have never been appraised),

(e) the perceived effectiveness of the current appraisal system,

(f) the level of training and back-up help which has been available to develop appraisal and counselling skills,

(g) perceptions of how well or badly the process is handled.

Such a mechanism for eliciting the views of people could involve a combination of a 'postal' survey and some face to face interviews.

Step 4. Evaluate the data collected and wherever possible express them visually, for example in graphs, histograms, or Pareto diagrams.

Step 5. Develop recommendations using the data which have been collected, having researched possible different methods, comparative costs, and timings. Build into the recommendations a timed and costed proposal where appropriate. Use the devil's advocate technique to check out the proposal.

Step 6. Prepare a management presentation and back-up report.

Step 7. Give the presentation and draw up an action plan on the basis of the ensuing discussion.

Step 8. Be responsible for tracking progress. Make sure that people do as they say they will do.

This group should be given up to fourteen weeks to present its findings. Meetings should be held as necessary to progress the work but should not average more than once a week. Meeting length should average one hour and should never exceed two hours. Action minutes must be produced as a result of each meeting. As far as possible the meetings should be organized into a regular pattern to avoid unnecessary time being spent coordinating people's diaries.

Aspect 3—Training and Development

One of the dimensions of the appraisal and goal-setting process will usually be a review of the training requirements for the particular manager or supervisor being worked with. The objective here is to continue the development and broadening of his skills. It is no good having elaborate mechanisms for selection, goal setting, appraisal, and counselling if we have not the means of helping people to improve in their weak areas, and further to develop their strengths. As such an organized and successful methodology for training and development is the third essential ingredient of equipping management for Excellence. IBM spend over half a billion dollars a year on training and they are not alone amongst the excellent large companies. Their commitment to training is legendary and, because they do it properly, is one of the key ingredients in their success. Training, however, needs to involve much more than simply sending people on courses if it is to have any real and lasting effect.

Enormous sums are spent yearly on management training and development, but recent surveys indicate that less than a third of top and middle managers feel that they learned important managerial skills through formal training, whether conducted within their own organization, using internal staff, or utilizing outside courses and consultants. The figure for 'in-house' training looks particularly bleak at under 10 per cent. Other disturbing figures are that less than half the managers attending courses received any briefing prior to the course, only 8 per cent were given any indication of the results expected from their attendance, and only half were consulted by their boss or training manager as to their immediate reaction on return. These indications are very alarming, yet the problem does not seem to be so much the course content itself.

There are two underlying problems, the first of which is that people are often sent on a course with scant regard for its appropriateness to the particular circumstances of the company and the individual managers who were designated to attend it at that time. Secondly, training is too often seen in isolation. Sending people on courses *per se* has only limited value, and most of the lessons learned are usually quickly forgotten as the realities of the 'back home' situation re-emerge. What is needed is a thought-through strategy not only for training but for training and development. Development, in this context, we define as 'assisted practice in the workplace'. In other words, we are looking ultimately, not for managers who know all the theories but do nothing with them, but for managers who know what they should do in theory and also who are able to do it in practice. The practical ability is of course the key one, when it is based on sound principles, and yet is very often forgotten when it comes to providing help. Given the choice between a classroom trainer on the payroll and a developer or facilitator, whose job it is to help people apply their learning in the real world, always choose the latter; he will pay for himself many times over.

In many organizations training is viewed simply as sending people on courses, in others training means organizing internal courses for all the managers 'because it is cheaper that way'. Excellent companies recognize that the human resource, like any other, needs continuing investment if it is to achieve and maintain a high degree of effectiveness. They also recognize that the investment needs to be designed appropriately to the present and future needs of the organization, and that these needs are for effective management in general and effective behaviour in planning, organizing, and controlling the resources within its control in a more specific sense.

An audit team will be needed to look into the current status of training and development within the organization. This group may well be most effectively constituted as a selection of middle managers and supervisors from different parts of the company. If this is decided, however, it will be important for the group to elicit the views of senior management and to include them in the findings.

In some circumstances it may be better not to have the training manager as a member of this group. This, hopefully, would help to avoid the possible danger that the only purpose of the group is to justify the system as it now is. Of course it will be essential to elicit his views and to build them in as part of the work, because he will need to 'own' whatever proposals are accepted. There is also a vital need to avoid the danger of leaving him feeling exposed and threatened.

This group should number no more than five people and the brief which is given to members should be to investigate the current status and effectiveness of training and development activities within the organization, and to highlight any changes in direction or additional dimensions which appear to be needed to equip the management team in the organization to achieve Excellence, now and in the future. It should be made clear that this group is not being asked to produce details of designing or specifying training programmes or the training plan; it is looking more at the general direction of training and development in the particular context of the organization in question.

It is recommended that the group work within the following broad guide-lines:

Step 1. Clarify mutual understanding of the brief and agree group norms to be used during meetings.

Step 2. Having read the relevant portion of this chapter, discuss its appropriateness to the organization at its present stage of development. Record details of the consensus.

Step 3. Gather data about the perceptions people have regarding the training and development they have or have not received. Include broad subject areas if appropriate and also people's views about the extent to which they have been able to put training lessons to practical use. This may be best achieved by a simple questionnaire backed up by some short discussions with a cross-section of people. If this method is used, include senior management in the survey.

Step 4. Gather data about the actual training and development which has been carried out in the organization. It would be advisable to get this information from the training department and specifically from the training manager. Make sure the training manager does not feel his position to be undermined or threatened.

Step 5. Highlight any major gaps between what happens and what people perceive, and also in the views people have about the effectiveness of training received and the reasons for this, both positive and negative.

Step 6. Plan a management presentation and put together a brief report summarizing the group's work.

Step 7. Present to management, and draw up an action plan as a result of the ensuing discussion.

Step 8. Track progress as required to do so by top management.

This group should be able to complete its report within fourteen weeks. The frequency and duration of meetings will probably need to be variable but should not average more than once a week for an hour. Action minutes must be produced at every meeting and the meetings should be scheduled as far as possible on a regular basis to avoid complicated diary planning on a week to week basis.

Chapter 6

COMMUNICATION

Excellent organizations genuinely want to hear the views of employees. Furthermore, they want to pass on, in a clear way, important messages from senior levels. Excellent organizations cannot survive as Excellent without having mechanisms for doing this. It is convenient to divide discussion in this section into three parts, to do with upward, downward, and lateral communication, but before we discuss each of these it is appropriate to introduce and discuss the concept which is commonly known as two-way communication.

Two-way communication is the most important of all the categories, since it implies and means that people are really talking with each other, rather than simply receiving messages on a one-way transmitter or holding what is know as collective monologues. Collective monologues occur with distressing frequency in organizations and are characterized by two people who apparently are having a dialogue (two-way communication) but in fact are holding two separate monologues. One person speaks about subject A, pauses, and then the second person speaks about subject B, pauses, then the first person continues where he left off, with subject A, and so it goes on. Anyone who has listened to politicians being interviewed, or children talking, knows the phenomenon. Unfortunately, as has been said, it is rife in organizations as well.

To develop an effective two-way communication system is one of the keys to achieving Excellence but unfortunately it is not quite as easy as saying that we want it to happen. In the past organizations have tried to 'introduce' two-way communication, and mechanisms have been invented to try and assist this process. It does not work like this. To achieve effective two-way communication requires much more than a technique. To have an open relationship with an individual requires more than the ability to speak; it requires that we believe we will be listened to, that we have confidence that what we say will not be used against us, that we believe the other party has a genuine interest in what we have to say, and so on. These are not things that we can legislate. We cannot force people, for example, to be genuinely interested in what we say. As such we cannot 'introduce' two-way communication, but what we can do is to work on developing an environment within which it not only becomes possible but it actually happens. Many of the particular activities which form a part of the Journey to Excellence are designed to help build this kind of environment, activities such as Quality Circles, Quality Department Groups, Quality Improvement Teams, and Quality Task Forces, which are dealt with elsewhere in this book. Furthermore, the whole of the Journey to Excellence can be seen as one in which we are attempting to make this kind of communication possible, not only between individuals but also between departments and between levels of the organization.

Downward communication

Any Excellent organization needs to communicate clearly with its people and, what is more, to do so in a regular fashion and in a way which reflects the normal way of life of the company. Annual 'jamborees' held in expensive hotels or cinemas to explain company performance and to generate or to regenerate interest and excitement are all very well, but they are not enough in their own right to fuel anyone's requirement for knowledge and understanding of what is happening in the organization. The vast majority of people really do want to know what is happening in their organization; furthermore, they would like to know on a very regular basis, and certainly much more frequently than once a year.

Department meetings are specifically designed to fill this need. They can be held at any level of frequency from daily (the Japanese model) to monthly, depending on the particular situation. Unfortunately, often the very mention of the subject of department meetings brings forth cries of boredom, or horror, and protestation that 'they have been tried before and they don't work'. This comment, however, always says more about the way they have been done than about the idea itself. To be effective, department meetings must not become a hollow ritual. No one likes wasting time, so the meetings have to be both interesting and useful. To achieve this requires competence in meeting the needs of members of staff, and having worthwhile things to say.

The first requirement is the subject of training for supervisors and managers and the second is a function of how open the organization is prepared to be in sharing information. Excellent companies operate a high trust policy and so are prepared to share more information with employees than are other organizations. Organizations that operate on a 'need to know' basis tend to get a majority of 'don't need to know', 'not my problem' staff. Additionally they always get very frustrated staff. Excellent organizations share information as freely and readily as it is possible to. People generally understand the need for some things to be confidential, so we do not need to talk about total openness since this does not make sense to most people. The message here is, however, that we should be actively seeking for information to pass down, taking 'trust risks' in doing so, rather than trying to estimate what is the least amount of information that we can get away with passing on.

A vivid example which illustrates the importance of this aspect of communcation happened in a large retail chain. When the proposal was made to share trading information with staff in the stores the initial reaction was an horrified rejection. It was explained that shopping areas are small places, that staff often had relatives working for competitors in the same street, and that they could well betray such confidences. The conversation continued:

'How much are your branch managers expected to know about the competition?'

'Everything they can, of course.'

'Do they get to know much?'

'Quite a bit.'

'What would an average, not excellent, branch manager know about the competition locally?'

'Oh, well, I suppose turnover, staffing, special offers policy, margins—stuff like that.'

'How do they get to know this information?'

'Well you develop a feel for it after a while.'

'So your managers know all this about the competition. What do you think they know about you?'

'Ah, well, yes, maybe they know something as well!!!'

The organization in question subsequently introduced a policy of open declaration and discussion of store trading results on a weekly basis with all staff, full and part time, for one division of its stores. After nine months they conducted an attitude survey to compare results between the test division and other parts of the company, and demonstrated dramatic and statistically significant differences in terms of understanding of the basic driving forces in the business, morale, satisfaction, and performance. The policy of open sharing of information had worked and worked extremely well.

One simple example illustrates the point in detail. In one medium-sized store, staff became interested particularly in the trading figures they were being shown, because they did not seem to fit with the preconceived notion held by members of staff. Further explanation and exploration revealed that staff were under the illusion that most of the money which was put in the till at the checkout points was profit! This meant, for example, that when a breakage occurred in the storeroom at the back, no one bothered too much because it was such a small amount in relation to 'all the profit going through the tills'. Once it was explained and demonstrated that only a tiny proportion of the turnover was profit, staff in this store became almost obsessive trying to control costs wherever it was in their ability to do so.

The conclusion is clear: a part of Excellence is having an effective mechanism for relaying information down the organization, not by relying on 'the grapevine' but by instituting an organized and regular procedure for holding meetings at an appropriate frequency. Of course it is not just as simple as introducing a technique or mechanism. Many organizations have assumed so and have found that their system has failed very quickly. In practice it is the skills of the managers who put over the messages that determine whether or not the whole system will be a success. It is essential that managers be trained in how to brief staff. Failure will always result if this is not done.

Upward communication

Many managers insist that they need no organized mechanism to provide the opportunity for employees to give feedback up the line. Such people often claim to operate an 'open door' policy. 'My people can come and see me at any time, my door is always open,' they say. Unfortunately this often means, in practice, that whereas the door is indeed open in a physical sense, there is perceived to be a six inch plate glass shield in the doorway, which is a far more effective deterrent to any entry than the door itself! It is very dangerous to rely on such informal systems. An organization striving for Excellence actively wants to hear the views of employees, positive and negative. They are a key instrument in the improvement process. The key word here is 'actively'. Unless organizations make it easy to hear and actually do hear such views, they will seriously inhibit themselves as they progress on the journey.

There are two mechanisms which many Excellent companies utilize in fostering upward communication and which should be standard. The first is the opinion survey. This is a device for collecting information from all staff on a regular basis. It gives the organization feedback about current views and opinions on a range of relevant subjects and also 'trend data' to track any changes of view over a period of time. Opinion surveys should be conducted on a regular basis, every six months is a sensible period, and should gather data from all staff. They should be designed by the particular organization with its own situation in mind, and many of the questions will be standard to ensure that trends can be extracted. The standard questions will usually relate to perceptions of morale, productivity, quality, involvement, general satisfaction, and so on. A further great beauty of conducting regular opinion surveys, however, is that they provide a regular opportunity for collecting data about additional issues as well, and the opportunity should not be missed since it can give valuable clues which can help in developing strategy on the Journey to Excellence.

The basic design of the survey should be the work of a Quality Task Force led by the

Quality director, but with advice from experts in the field of questionnaire design. It is all too easy to design such instruments with in-built bias, simply due to lack of experience in such matters. To save time and effort the questionnaire should be designed so that the results can be entered directly into a computer for analysis, and individual contributions should be anonymous since this will help facilitate openness and honesty in the which people give feedback. It is important, however, that though names are not capable of being identified departments are, since the data can provide valuable insights and feedback to help individual managers. Once the results of the survey are known they should be published openly so that members of staff can see them and can explore them in detail, if they so desire.

The second mechanism which is important for collecting upward feedback, particularly of a negative nature, is a system which enables staff who feel they have been badly treated to report the matter. The system needs to be organized so that such reports are sent to a suitably senior manager. In large companies this may be the head of a division or a major plant whereas in smaller companies it would be the chief executive. It is an important feature of any such mechanism that there is the 'right of appeal', ultimately to the chief executive of the organization no matter what its size. With such systems it is, of course, utterly essential that every such complaint should be taken seriously and investigated thoroughly, in a common and systematic way. It is not sufficient with such mechanisms to rely on informal arrangements. Such systems need to be thought through in a lot of detail. The procedures and format need to be clearly understood by everyone, not only for making the complaint in the first place but also for investigating it once it has been made. Some managers become very anxious at the thought of such mechanisms in their company, but really no one who is behaving in a fair and reasonable manner has anything to fear since any abuse of the system, by the occasional member of staff, is invariably spotted very quickly. The importance of having such a mechanism is that it gives every member of staff the clear message that they have a right to be treated fairly according to the stated philosophy of the company, and furthermore that the organization is utterly committed to ensuring that this happens in practice.

A third mechanism for gathering upward information concerns the positive suggestions that people in the organization have. Such mechanisms are commonly known as suggestion schemes. Many organizations have tried suggestion schemes and have found, after an intial flurry of activity for a few months, that they fizzle out. This will always tend to happen if such mechanisms are introduced as self-standing entities. It is interesting that suggestion schemes stand the test of time in Excellent organizations, and the reason for this is that they are seen by everyone as one dimension of a whole process; they are not introduced as something in their own right. Some of the big Excellent corporations receive phenomenal numbers of suggestions from staff each and every year, to the extent that they require substantial numbers of staff in suggestion departments to handle the volume of work involved in receiving and evaluating ideas and rewarding the originator. Before we throw up our hands at the thought of employing staff for such work, let us remember that Toyota claim that at least 25 per cent of its net profit annually comes directly from these ideas! Furthermore, we should remember that any such scheme shares the benefits of the suggestion with the originator if the idea is introduced; they are always designed so that both the organization and the employee 'win'. When organized well, and as a part of the whole process, the winnings invariably reward both handsomely.

Many proposals which are received with suggestion schemes are directly linked to saving money or making things more productive, and can be evaluated in financial terms. Other ideas which are still welcomed and rewarded relate to less tangible aspects of the organization, but aspects nonetheless which can assist us on the Journey to Excellence. Some organizations have different types of award for different suggestions and there is considerable scope for creativity in the design of such schemes.

Lateral communication

One of the problems with the way that most businesses are structured is that people tend to be put into functional 'drainpipes'. This tends to have a number of unfortunate side effects. One, for example, is that it tends to reinforce the natural human tendency to point fingers at others. So typically we get the 'If only the engineers did their job right' or 'It's the sales force's fault' syndrome. This is a negative feature of organizational life in most companies but one which it is important to recognize. People usually tend to relate to their own department and their own function, up and down the organization. This feature is reinforced by the fact that promotions tend largely to be within technical specializations. It is interesting that many Excellent companies deliberately break this pattern by encouraging people to make lateral moves and by assigning people to jobs outside their functional specialization. This occurs particularly at management levels where the basic rules and process of managing can be seen as being pretty similar whatever the tasks being performed in the department.

A further problem with functional organizations is that the process of work actually goes across functional boundaries. An order is picked up by sales who pass it to planning. They send it to production, who make the product, and pass it to distribution. The paperwork is sent from them to accounts who invoice the customer. This is not to say that functional organizations are wrong, merely that we have to be careful in managing the logical and human outcomes of this way of organizing.

In most organizations, therefore, there will be a need for creating opportunities for lateral communication both at the same level and at different levels. Of course, there are sometimes mechanisms already available, for example sports and social clubs, but often these are extra-curricula. What is needed are possibilities within the main framework of the work itself. A number of the activities within the Journey to Excellence model specifically encourage cross-functional working and collaboration, for example quality task forces and quality improvement teams, which are discussed elsewhere in this book. At the outset quality task forces will be particularly important, as will the audit teams that are set up to look at the organizational basics.

Though it is vital to promote opportunities for lateral communication it is dangerous to rush too quickly into setting up a lot of Quality Improvement Teams, or Quality Task Forces, since there is an ever-present danger that the finger-pointing habit will have a negative effect on the work. What is required first is that we get out of this habit and focus on 'putting our own house in order'. The phasing of the activities which go to make up the Journey to Excellence are dealt with later in the book. Suffice it to say here that there are a number of opportunities which encourage productive lateral communication. Some need to be built in early in the process and others play a fuller part later in the piece.

The subject of communication is one which certainly needs to be dealt with by an audit team. It will be fundamental to success that the organization is able to develop a really effective system which will ensure that the messages which are passed up, down, and sideways are open, honest, and constructive. Clearly it is an aspect which requires working on constantly and the work of the audit team will help to structure the requirement both initially and into the future. One difficulty which the audit teams will face is the tendency in many organizations to lay many different types of problem at the door of 'poor communication'. The group will need to be able to be more precise than this and to break the word 'communication' into parts which can be more readily handled. Simply doing this will help to separate aspects which are genuinely related to communication from those which are, in fact, different.

There is no one way of viewing the component parts of communication. In this chapter we have looked at downward, upward, lateral, and two-way communication. Each of these could be split down in all manner of ways, for example written, visual, verbal, by department, between departments, and so on. The audit team is not being asked to go to this level of detail at this stage. The subject is such a huge one that it would be all too easy to get lost in it. At this stage what is required in our effort to achieve excellence is an analysis of what happens currently in the categories which have been discussed in this chapter and also a proposal of the requirement for the future, together with a recommendation for handling the requirement.

Since communication is fundamental to all levels of the organization the audit team needs to be able to represent everyone, and as such this group needs to include people from all levels of the organization. The reality of communication is what people perceive it to be. Many organizations have apparently sound mechanisms which they appear to use, yet people in the organization percieve that the mechanisms do not exist. It is essential in the work of this group that the perceptions of different levels in the organization are gathered and that these are taken into account in forming any proposals for improvement. All the audit teams need to be small groups, simply to avoid the problems and difficulties which inevitably come about when a group has more than about ten members, and this group is no different. Since it is important to get a rounded view, however, this group can be placed at the top end of the range and have nine or ten members if the size of the organization and the number of levels warrants it. The work of this group will need to include information collected from staff. It will be particularly important to be careful in the design of any questionnaire or survey since it is easy with this subject to get tangled up in semantics. Since the word communication can often mean very different things to different people great care is needed to be sure that any information collected means what it appears to mean. The brief for this audit team is to investigate current mechanisms which are used for communication within the organization and to propose any alterations and additions that are required to equip the organization for Excellence. The recommendation should include the proposed method for planning and introducing any new aspect.

The group should be encouraged to work through the following broad stages:

Step 1. Establish a common understanding of the brief and agree norms to be used during group meetings.

Step 2. Having read this chapter come to a view about the relevance of the broad subjects covered, i.e. upward, downward, lateral, and two-way communication. Record details of the consensus.

Step 3. Design a mechanism for collecting information from staff about relevant aspects of communication as it works currently in the organization. Remember the cautions noted in the text when doing this.

Step 4. Collect information about the mechanisms currently in use both in theory and in practice.

Step 5. If possible, research concepts of potential interest by contacting other organizations who use them and gathering their views. Also gather other information that may be available on these different subjects.

Step 6. Establish priorities.

Step 7. Agree appropriate ways of following up recommended mechanisms, for example by setting up a quality task force to work on the issue, by getting quotes from outside consultants, by getting internal resources to manage the item.

Step 8. Develop the package of recommendations, complete with an assessment of costs and benefits. Agree on a proposed method of managing any work which is agreed. Check that the whole proposal is feasible in the real world. Remember that too much too soon is as bad as too little too late!

Step 9. Prepare a management presentation and report.

Step 10. Give the management presentation and formulate an action plan on the basis of the ensuing discussion.

Step 11. Track results if this role is given to the group. Ensure that people do as they say they will do.

This subject involves a major piece of work and will probably take longer than the subjects being covered by the other audit teams. It is recommended that eighteen weeks be allocated to the management presentation. It could be that this group might wish to break the job down into smaller and more manageable pieces at an early stage and to set up subgroups or even different groups. If so the timing and the stages will change, but a time limit should be set before the start of any group. The meetings will need to vary in frequency and length but should not average much more than once a week and for one hour. No meeting should last longer than two hours. Action minutes must be produced as a result of every meeting. It will be advisable as far as possible to try and schedule the meetings into a regular pattern at the outset, since this saves time in coordinating diaries and room availability. It is usually easier to cancel a meeting than to organize one.

Chapter 7

CUSTOMER ORIENTATION

One of the dangers with the topic of customer orientation is that all too often it is treated in a trite, skin-surface fashion which does no justice to its importance on the Journey to Excellence. Quite simply, without it there is no way we can achieve our goal, since real customer orientation and Excellence go together hand in glove. Many organizations purport to be customer oriented and point to posters around their offices and factories—posters which say things like 'The customer is king' and 'The customer pays our wages'. There is, of course, nothing wrong with such methods of highlighting the importance of the subject, as long as they form part of an overall strategy. Simply putting posters up, however, will achieve next to nothing, yet unfortunately this is what so often happens. Another fairly recent innovation has built on the recognition that customers tend to like being treated nicely. This has come like a bolt from the blue to many organizations who have often rushed off and organized a whole series of so-called 'smiling courses' to teach employees to do just that. Again, there is nothing intrinsically wrong with such activities, indeed they are important, it is just that the 'have a nice day' syndrome, as it is commonly known, will benefit us nothing unless it is put within a much wider framework and context.

The first essential recognition that everyone in the organization must come to if we are to achieve anything approaching Excellence is that customers are not only the people who ultimately buy the goods and services we provide. These are our external customers, and important of course they are, since ultimately they do pay our wages. One of the difficulties that many employees have, however, is that this external customer seems a very distant being. If someone's job requires that he welds two pieces of metal together, or checks expenses claims, or drives a fork-lift truck in a warehouse, or works in the accounts office, it is sometimes very difficult to get a real picture of the customer. He seems to be a long way off. To make a pair of shoes involves more than a hundred pairs of hands, and many products are far more complex than this. It is hardly surprising, therefore, that sometimes people within the process feel that they are distant from and have no clear perception of the end user.

Less understandably but very commonly, it is also a fact that many people who do actually deal directly with the end user have little notion of what he wants and how he should be treated. As an exercise, go through a week and tally up the times you have contacted a person or an organization, with you as the end user, and out of those times the proportion where you were really treated well (like a 'king'), the times when you were treated adequately but no more, and the times when you were treated less than adequately. It is staggering the occasions that fall into the last two categories. The telephone operator takes two minutes to answer, the hotel receptionist looks at you as if there is something wrong with you, the supermarket checkouts have queues ten people deep, the insurance company forget to send you a claim form, the airline staff take half an hour to serve a drink and then pile the different courses of your meal onto the tray all at the same time. All in the space of a week, and not an unusual week either! Unfortunately, most people have developed well-tuned defence mechanisms to withstand the assault and this leads to a real tragedy, which is that we do not give feedback often enough. It is sometimes said that for every one dissatisfied customer who actually writes a letter of complaint, there are a hundred who do not bother. If customer relations departments used the larger figures for their statistics it would put their jobs into a rather different context.

As far as we are concerned on our Journey to Excellence, it really is essential that the service we give to our customers is first rate, not as an isolated activity but as a part of the whole process. There is little doubt that all staff will require training in this aspect of their work. Contact with the end user is a complex affair and can involve difficult types of communication which people need to be trained in. It seems a bizarre omission that people who deal with customers are always trained in the technicalities of their jobs, yet often not in the skills of actually using the phone, writing a letter, talking face to face, and so on.

All of these aspects need covering since organizations can usually improve the interface with their end users very significantly and to great mutual benefit. This whole aspect of the journey, however, even with this aspect covered, still seems to be rather unsatisfactory.

This is because it is one thing to ensure that those people who deal with the end user are competent both technically and also in the process of dealing with that person or organization but this really is only half the battle since we are still left with the majority of staff in our organization who do not deal with the customer directly. Thus far we have done little to assist them as far as this vital topic is concerned, and, frankly, even with those who do have the direct contact, we have not done anything except to scratch the surface of the requirement. The training which we can provide is valid and valuable and the exhortations are appropriate, but we need much more.

The key to developing a real understanding of this aspect of the Journey to Excellence is the notion of the internal customer. Customers, for Excellent companies, are not only people we sell things to. In fact everyone in the organization both is a customer and has customers as a result of the work he does. These customers are exactly the same in degree of importance as the external users we have already dealt with, the only difference being that they are people within the organization. Specifically, the internal customer is the person who receives our work after we have done our job. Similarly, we are the customer of the person who passes the work to us after he has done his job. Everything that is done in the organization can be looked at in this way, and if it is, the whole concept of customer orientation changes instantaneously and becomes a vital ingredient in everyone's job.

What we are left with, then, is the job of demonstrating to people that this is the case, of persuading people that the internal customer is as important as the external customer, and of training people in the skills required to deal with customers. The training that is needed is exactly the same as that relevant to training in external customer orientation; there is not a syllable of difference in the skills required and so we can, as of now, forget the distinction between internal and external and refer to both simply as customers.

'The customer is king' is the slogan on many posters. We now have a vastly different perspective on this lofty thought, because it now means that Joe or Jack is king. Joe and Jack, of course, are the people who are always complaining about the work we send them because, according to them, we do not understand their problems. From today, when they say this, it is exactly the same as the telephone operator, the supermarket manager, the hotel receptionist, and so on, saying to us, 'You are wrong to criticize, you don't understand my problems!'

This concept represents a very big change for most people and will require not only a different way of thinking but of behaving as well, and as such it is not a change that is likely to be made overnight. Most of us will need reminding on a regular basis, and also helping for a period of time until it becomes second nature. This will be a role played by the Quality director and the other resources allocated to guide our way on this journey. The details of the basic training which is necessary to initiate this change are given in a later chapter of this book, as are some of the mechanisms which will help employees not only to understand but to live this concept in their working lives.

This topic may or may not require an audit team to look at it. The key questions which need to be answered here are, firstly, to what extent the company is structured in a way which promotes closeness to the end user amongst most staff, or distance from him. Secondly, what level of skills do we think currently exist in dealing with all facets of our relationship with the end user. Thirdly, we need to know to what extent the concept of the internal customer is understood and to what extent is it an organized and formal part of the way we do things. In some organizations the answers to these questions will be very clear without needing to set up a team to research them. If this is the case then there is no point in wasting peoples' time answering questions that have already been answered; we should get on with the task of retraining people and helping them to live this new philosophy from day to day.

If an audit team is felt to be appropriate it should be a relatively small group of four or five people from different levels of the organization. The brief is to assess the current level of customer orientation in the organization and to highlight key areas of concern. The broad steps involved in this are as follows:

Step 1. Agree a common understanding of the brief and establish norms to be used during the work of the group.

Step 2. Having read this chapter, come to a view about its relevance to the organization in question.

Step 3. Map the organization in a way which demonstrates how near or far people are from the end customer in terms of structure; for example how many steps are there between staff and the end user? This can be done in conjunction with the organization structure group. Alternatively, their work can be 'borrowed' to avoid duplication of effort.

Step 4. Critically examine the likely reaction of outside users to the service they are given. Utilize current data and gather data as appropriate. Do not point fingers at individuals; often the organization 'forces' people to give bad service or at least does not train people to do it properly.

Step 5. Assess the level of understanding of the concept of the internal customer and the extent to which it is a formal part of the way we do things.

Step 6. Establish priorities for action.

Step 7. Prepare a management presentation and report.

Step 8. Give the presentation and record actions agreed.

Step 9. Track progress. Ensure that people do as they say they will do.

This group should be given fourteen weeks to complete its work. The group should not need to meet more than weekly and the meetings should not last more than one hour. Action minutes must be produced as a result of every meeting and the meetings should be organized to a regular pattern to avoid unnecessary time being wasted in coordinating diaries.

Chapter 8

'OWNERSHIP'

Excellence both requires and implies the active commitment of all employees. This in turn cannot be a one-way contract. One of the most demoralizing aspects of so many companies is the realization, when it comes, that all of the hard work, the extra unpaid hours, the anxious worrying over decisions, in other words the intense commitment that has been given over a long period of time, was only a one-way deal, that the company feels no sense of commitment to the employee and will be prepared to drop him without so much as a 'by your leave'. Organizations that think of and treat their people in this way will not be able to achieve and sustain Excellence because they will not carry enough commitment from their employees to sustain the activities that are required.

We need not, in this context, be talking about guaranteed lifetime employment, though it is rather interesting to observe that some of the truly Excellent companies have just such a system. What is required is that employees are able to feel a sense of ownership of the organization. There are different ways of achieving this and there is no one formula which is right in all cases. It is essential, however, that such a sense of ownership exists and is built on.

The first possibility for developing such an ownership would be actually to give employees the chance of becoming shareholders in the organization. An increasing number of companies do have share option schemes, and these can and do work well in the context of developing higher levels of ownership and commitment. This is not to say that such a system would be appropriate or even possible for every organization. Clearly it would be inappropriate for many privately owned companies and, of course, nationalized industries.

A second option which will probably be more appropriate for many will be to try to develop ownership through the creation of a 'high performance, high reward' environment. Wherever possible this should become a part of the strategy. This should not be taken to imply that people are only interested in economic gain, because it is clearly not the case, given that the other circumstances surrounding the employment are dealt with effectively. Equally, since the benefits which accrue from Excellence are large, it is appropriate that they be shared with the employees, since it will be they that have made the organization Excellent. The role of money as a motivator has taken up a huge amount of time for researchers and trainers, as well as managers, over the past three decades, and the work has been useful in many ways. Summarizing the results it does appear that people's performance will improve when it is directly instrumental in achieving higher wages, gaining promotion, or producing an increased acceptance by co-workers. In each case the relationship is strongest for those who value the outcome most. What we are aiming at on our Journey to Excellence is an environment in which participation, often on a voluntary basis, becomes the accepted norm. As this is achieved and reinforced and as the positive results associated with this participation begin to accrue it will be more and more possible to recognize success through money.

A question here, of course, is whether or not such recognition should be fixed, in other words be an addition to the basic wage, or whether it should be variable. Motivation theory points in the direction of variable payments depending on results, and as a matter of interest this is very much the Japanese model, where generally speaking a considerable proportion of the payment package is variable, reflecting the performance of the organization.

There are very many ways of organizing such payment structures. At one end of the spectrum there are profit-sharing arrangements and at the other there are a whole range of bonus systems which can be introduced. Here is not the place for a detailed treatise on the possible mechanisms; there are organizations which specialize in the detailed design of such matters. It is necessary, however, for the organization seeking Excellence to consider the extent to which it wishes to promote high levels of commitment and ownership, at least in part through its payment structure. Whatever people's differing beliefs are concerning the role of pay as a positive motivator, there is common agreement that it is very damaging to get the strategy wrong and as a generalization it will pay most organizations to work towards a 'high pay, high performance' environment.

The third dimension, which will be relevant to every organization seeking Excellence, concerns a very different kind of ownership, commonly called 'psychological ownership'. We have already stated that it is far too simplistic in the vast majority of cases to assume their people are solely interested in economic gain. People at work have a whole range of needs that require satisfying and an important dimension of Excellence will be the extent to which the organization satisfies these needs. Two essential aspects of this are worth reviewing at this stage.

The first concerns one particular need that people bring to work with them—the need for achievement. Some have this at a higher level than others, of course, but it is an unusual employee that does not have it at all. Indeed, if people do not appear to be interested in achievement it is more likely that this is telling us something about the organization than the people in it. Clearly the Journey to Excellence is a long and difficult one. It is immensely challenging for every member of staff, and it needs to be explained as such; there is no point in saying that it will be easy. A singular beauty of the Journey to Excellence is that it will help to satisfy the need for achievement of staff because the different activities which make up the journey provide plenty of scope for people to achieve success in tasks which are difficult and challenging. This in its own right will develop a degree of psychological ownership.

The second essential aspect concerns participation. People who are given the opportunity to participate in making decisions which affect them perform at a higher level, and with more commitment, than those who are not given the opportunity. Again, since the mechanisms used in achieving Excellence stress the participation and involvement of all employees, we are in good shape to meet this need as well. It could be said that the Journey to Excellence progressively creates psychological ownership because of the mechanisms it uses, and maybe this is one of the main reasons why it is such a powerful process.

In summary, then, it is clear that for Excellence to be achieved there is a need for all employees to feel a sense of ownership. In an ideal world we would be able to utilize all of the mechanisms for achieving this, including offering part of the actual ownership of the organization, profit sharing, or other means of establishing a 'high pay, high performance' environment, and finally creating meaningful levels of psychological ownership. In reality not all organizations will be able, or willing, to use all of these facets. Where this is the case it will be essential to remember that, in the longer term, people will have to feel that it is worth their while if they are to give and to maintain their commitment. This 'something' does not have to be tangible money reward, though this will help, but it does have to include a feeling that it is worth while from the point of view of getting things done, being involved in a way which uses their talents, and being recognized for the contributions made.

This subject can be a difficult one to investigate using an audit team, and in some cases it would be inappropriate to do so. Sometimes it will be more necessary for the team to be established to look specifically into one or other aspect. For example it would be appropriate in many organizations to decide on an investigation of different types of bonus schemes as a part of the strategy for developing high levels of ownership. On other occasions it will be very important to investigate the aspect of psychological ownership. In many organizations there is all too often a tendency for people to make broad and generalized statements about important issues such as morale, which often have a direct bearing on the extent of the feelings of ownership in employees. This is of course very dangerous, and the established methodology used by the audit teams is immensely valuable in replacing these opinion-based statements with organized factual analysis. The audit teams are designed to avoid becoming 'talking groups'. They are structured, and assisted, with a view to ensuring that things get done as a result of their work, and thus they are an immensely powerful way of handling this stage of the journey, since they recognize that people, in general, are very busy and do not have time to spend on fruitless debate.

This audit team will, generally speaking, consist of senior managers and often will include senior union representatives. The group itself should not be a big one; in normal circumstances only four or five people should be invited to work on the issue. The precise brief for this group will depend on the formal mechanisms which are already in place relating to the subject and may need to include a review of the effectiveness of such mechanisms. In many circumstances there will not be any formal structures in place for developing ownership and the audit team may be required to investigate different possibilities as a part of its work. The one subject that will always need looking at, however, is that of 'psychological ownership'. The brief given to this group should be to investigate the current mechanisms that are in place which encourage or detract from the development of high levels of ownership, to assess the current level of psychological ownership, and to report with recommendations on practical ways of developing higher levels of ownership at all levels of the organization.

The broad structure that the group should be encouraged to follow in its work is as follows:

Step 1.   Clarify mutual understanding of the brief and agree group norms to be used in the meetings.

Step 2.   Having read this chapter, discuss its content and come to an agreement about its relevance and importance in this organization. Agree any limitations which will affect the possible recommendations of this group, for example share option schemes would not be possible in a nationalized industry! Record details of the consensus as far as relevance of the topic, its importance, and also any limitations in the particular organization.

Step 3.   Collect factual data specifically concerned with the issue of psychological ownership, but also about the perceptions of employees regarding the effectiveness of mechanisms currently in use to create a high pay, high performance environment. At this stage it is obviously important to be very careful in the design of any questionnaires which are used and in the structure of any interviews that are undertaken. This is because the issue is not easy to define and tie down precisely and it would be all too easy to become trapped by different interpretations of words.

Step 4.   Interpret the data carefully. Try to look at it from different angles in understanding it and the messages it contains.

Step 5. Use a technique such as force field analysis to investigate possible ways of improving the level of ownership felt by employees at different levels. What would be useful at one level might not be so beneficial at another.

Step 6. Form recommendations from the force field analysis or alternative analysis, and ensure that they are capable of being introduced in the real world.

Step 7. Prepare a management presentation and back-up report.

Step 8. Give the presentation and draw up an action plan on the basis of what is agreed during the discussion after the presentation.

Step 9. Track progress. Ensure that agreed actions are completed on time.

This group should be able to complete its work within ten weeks. The meetings held by the group should not last more than one hour, and should be held no more frequently than weekly. Action minutes must be produced as a result of every meeting and the meetings should be scheduled on a regular basis to avoid diary planning problems.

Chapter 9

TRUST

Someone said in a speech a few years ago, 'Trust, train and inform your people and they will reward you many times.' He was of course right, but words are simple to say; try convincing most managers and organizations to do anything about it! At best the vast majority pay lip service to such a notion, and for many the idea of trusting staff, or even managers, with anything except perhaps the most trivial and unimportant details is both foreign and anathema. Many top managers, if it comes down to it, would not trust their people further than they could throw them. Trust, however, is a basic requirement of the process of achieving Excellence, and so needs to be explored in some detail.

Why is trust so important? There are three main reasons, all of which require explanation. Firstly, we all know that the world is changing, and what is more changing at a rapidly increasing rate. Change is now just about the only constant in the world around us. This means that any organization wishing to keep up, forge ahead, or even survive, needs to be able not only to manage the consequences of change retrospectively and when it is forced on us, but to promote it actively—to be ahead of the game wherever possible. Rather like the Starship Enterprise in *Star Trek*, organizations increasingly have to 'go where no man has gone before'. If they want to survive they have no choice. All of this implies that new ideas, new products, new variations are needed. In a nutshell, innovation is essential.

The link between change and trust is twofold. Firstly, the creative process of exploring new possibilities is often very unstructured and needs to be so if the real creativity of those involved is to be tapped. Creativity requires an amount of chaos which is something of which businesses are usually very intolerant, and this can lead to all sorts of difficulties. The organization needs to be able to allow people in these roles a very wide range of freedom to experiment, explore, propose, and promote new ideas and possibilities. It involves specifying and giving a high level of freedom, and therefore trust, to those engaged in this aspect of the organization's activities. Innovation is key to the future. It cannot come out of a repressive environment except as revolution. Excellent organizations encourage innovation and innovative ideas, in deeds as well as words. In this way the organization constantly revolutionizes itself.

The second link between change and trust concerns the day to day behaviour of all staff. Change is not only apparent in the internal dynamics of the organization, it is everywhere. It affects every aspect of life in virtually every culture. The social dynamics of change very quickly affect organizational life and often the organization responds negatively and defensively. Not many years ago women were often sent home for wearing trousers to work. Crazy we may say, but are we much more understanding now? Examples abound of organizations that seem unable to cope with staff who are anything but safe conformists, whether it be to do with dress, general appearance, hair length, or behaviour. This is not a platform to promote minority types and preferences but it is nonetheless important that organizations stay abreast of the times not only within the technology of their industry but also with the social fabric of society. The reality today is that many individuals in society are becoming more demanding in terms of what they want from work and the psychological contract they make with their employer. This often sets up an equal and opposite defensive reaction on the part of the organization which falls back on 'old style' values, creating a win/lose situation which can quickly become the norm. What excellent organizations are able to do is to encourage people to speak their minds, to voice their opinions, to air their doubts, without there being an implicit assumption that such activities are negative and counterproductive. Excellent organizations want to hear the views of their people, as discussed in Chapter 6 of this book on the subject of communication.

To hear the voice of the people involves more than simply assuming that the opportunity is there, or even saying that it is. In many organizations the underlying message which is perceived by managers and staff alike is 'don't rock the boat'. Only the organization and its senior managers can change this, and it can only be done by demonstrating in practice that it is more worth while for employees to behave in a different way, to show in deeds that any questioning of the organization is not put down dismissively with the 'culprit' being branded a 'barrack room lawyer'. Some of the new high technology electronics companies have developed and refined such methods, and certainly they lead the way in this respect. There is still an equivalent need, however, in other organizations dealing with far less esoteric products and services.

This is not to say of course that every part of every organization should be based on loose, free-form structures and attitudes. Like everything these have their place alongside other more traditional ways of organizaing and behaving. In the 1960s so-called 'think tanks' became fashionable for a short period of time. They were improperly understood and introduced by many organizations and broadly speaking enjoyed only a short life. This is sad in many ways since if treated in the right way and with the right spirit, such mechanisms can be a partial answer to this need, even in the most conservative of organizations. Sadly they usually become rather mundane standing committees, conservatively talking about, and proposing, second-rate technical solutions to problems they were ill-equipped to tackle in the first place. They would have better served their masters, the top management of the organization, by being more stimulating and provocative, 'way out', and, yes, irreverent. Remember the tale of the Emperor's new clothes. Top managers everywhere are constantly told how wonderful is their new suit of clothes. It is only they that, over a period of time, can create an environment in which it is a realistic possibility for their subordinates to tell them that really they are naked! There are many advantages for the top manager if he can create this environment. Better to be told of our nakedness in time to do something about it than for it to become a public spectacle. It often happens. The reality of change and the requirement for trust go hand in glove.

In a fascinating study undertaken by one major corporation a clear correlation was revealed between managers who enjoyed high productivity and morale, low absenteeism, and sickness in their departments and those who imbued staff with a high level of trust, exemplified in allowing a wider range of decision making at staff level. In a word it was a vindication of the policy of delegation. A vital subset of the same research, however, revealed that it is very easy to confuse delegation with abdication. Successful delegation requires that staff are trained and developed to be able to take on the delegated responsibilities, and also that the manager is able to handle this management style. If it is attempted inappropriately the result can be not simply staying at the same point but taking a step backwards in all respects. It is a salutory warning to anyone who is playing games with this whole idea that the outcome, if it is found to be wrong in its motivation, can lead to a worse situation than the starting point.

In summary, then, the three main reasons why trust is so important are, firstly, to help promote innovation and innovative thinking amongst appropriate groups in the organization, secondly, to encourage a questioning attitude amongst all staff, and thirdly, to share the increasing burden of problem solving more widely amongst staff.

At this point we need to deal firmly with the accusation that some will level at this topic, which is that it can be equated with 'soft centred' management. A moment's thought will reveal that this is far from being 'soft'; in fact it is extremely hard in the sense both of being difficult to do and 'hard nosed' in a business sense. Firstly, anyone who thinks that trusting is easy should consider how easy it is to let a child go out on the public highway on a bicycle for the first time. This and the countless other examples that one can think of reveal, of course, that it is actually very difficult to let go in a parental sense. This is also the case in management. Trust involves risk and most of us are not noted for our risk taking; we prefer to play it safe. So 'soft' is actually 'hard', when it is done well.

This leads us to the next point, which is how do we deal with trust in a practical way? The key to this is that we are not proposing that everyone should be trusted with everything starting from now. This would be neither believable nor sensible. It is essential, however, that organizations are aware of the requirement for developing a high trust environment and that they commit themselves to moving in this direction progressively and over a period of time. The tools that are needed to make this a practical possibility are contained in the statement quoted at the start of this chapter, namely training and information. Before we trust our children to ride a bicycle on the public highway we make sure that they are trained in the technical sense in the mechanisms of riding a bike and also that they are informed about a range of things including the highway code, the most likely dangers, and the key 'do's and don't's'. It is a process that takes time, and is often very frustrating for parents and children alike. The analogy holds good with organizations. Excellent companies invest extensively in the training and education of staff at all levels, not because it is a nice thing to do, but because they know it will increase not only the level of knowledge but also the stock of decision making ability in the organization.

Furthermore, Excellent companies actively seek to share information with staff rather than to hide it. This subject is dealt with more fully in the chapter on communication (Chapter 6), but it is perhaps worth repeating here that organizations that operate a policy of only communicating what they think staff need to know, tend to get a lot of staff who do not want to know. So the practicalities of developing high trust as an organizational norm involve a policy of training and information. There may well be a minority of people in the organization who do not respond to the policy, either out of a lack of interest or because they are out of sympathy with the goals of the company. Where this is the case such people will represent a tiny minority and should not deter the management from its chosen course.

The final question to be answered here is what are the real benefits of developing such a policy? Again we can return to the quotation at the beginning of the chapter which says that if we develop a high level of trust through a policy of training and information sharing, then the people in the organization will 'reward you many times'. The reason for developing such a policy quite simply is that it will help contribute to the commercial success of the organization. This will come about through the increased range of skills staff bring to bear in their work and their improved ability in solving problems effectively, which makes more real delegation a practical possibility.

Delegation means that more problems will be solved successfully as more people are trusted to make decisions, and more minds will be working on opportunities for making things even better. Furthermore, the personal motivation and commitment of most staff will increase commensurate with the increased trust exhibited by the organization. This aspect is not to be ignored but it is to be kept in perspective. Trust, though it involves risk, tends not to be given until a reasonable level of confidence has been reached and it is sure that the trust will not be abused. Therefore, though management in the organization must initiate the process and follow it up, each additional quotient of trust depends directly on the response of staff to the previous one. The process therefore involves a delicate balance, though management should constantly be on the lookout for opportunities to take 'trust risks'.

Trust is not something that can really be audited in any formal way, though it should be the subject of serious thought and discussion, especially amongst senior managers from whom must come the first moves, and the ongoing commitment, to making it work.

Part 3

QUALITY—THE BRICKS AND MORTAR

Chapter 10

QUALITY ISN'T JUST QUALITY CONTROL

Quality is the bricks and mortar of Excellence. Without it, quite simply Excellence cannot be achieved and as such any organization interested in this concept must have a systematic and dedicated approach to the subject. Furthermore, this is not 'old style' Quality with the Quality Control department all dressed in their white coats. 'New Quality' involves a whole range of new concepts which form the basis of a revolutionary new approach when combined with the other features of the model. A large portion of any organization's Journey to Excellence will be taken up with issues to do with Quality and it is vital therefore that there is a sound understanding of what 'new Quality' is all about and what the differences are between it and more traditional approaches.

It all starts with the definition of the word. Ask yourself how you would define the word 'Quality'. Ask others around you and the chances are that Quality will emerge as a pretty imprecise notion involving such things as 'goodness', 'expensiveness', 'having class', 'satisfying'. There are a range of problems which surround these kind of definitions, basically to do with the fact that they are all capable of a very wide range of individual interpretations. This vagueness is at the root of many difficulties with traditional Quality concepts. With the new concept the definition of the word Quality becomes absolutely clear and standard. It is 'meeting the (stated) requirements of the customer, now and in the future'. The key difference here is that Quality by this definition is not only measurable, it has to be measured. Indeed, with this Quality concept we can say that if it is not measured then it is not Quality.

Another big change which affects this definition lies in the use of the word 'customer'. Traditionally, Quality directs itself to the dream of 'satisfied customers' defined as the end users of the goods or services. Here we broaden the definition significantly and include 'internal customers', who are the people that we supply with the product of our work. If we work on an assembly line, our customers may be the next people on the line. In an office it will similarly be the person we pass our work to. If we are a secretary, our customer will be our boss for much of the time. If we are a middle manager asked to write a report for the chief executive, then he is our customer in this instance, and for the rest of the job we may have a range of customers who use the output of our department. Most people have more than one customer and more than one 'supplier' (the person for whom we are the customer).

The practical realities of the word Quality change enormously with the inclusion of internal customers. All of a sudden Quality is not something that affects an end customer who is never seen and will never be known. It is not something that 'is not my job' but immediately becomes of importance to everyone in the organization since it is everyone's job to meet the requirements of their own particular customers. Clearly this will require a big change in many people's attitudes and behaviour, and one of the challenges of any Excellence process lies in effecting this. Traditionally Quality has been perceived as the preserve of a group of people in white coats who walked around the production floor and caused problems for production people! Though this may be somewhat of an exaggeration, it probably contains at least a grain of truth. Generally speaking employees have not felt, and do not feel, that Quality is their business. This does not mean that people are not interested in producing good work, just that the word Quality is usually interpreted as 'Quality Control', and since there is a department called that on the production side of the business, we assume that it is their job to look after it.

This broadening of Quality to include every employee is sometimes perceived as a threat by Quality Control departments. This is sad when it happens because the change really is not designed to threaten them. Indeed much of the useful work done by them in most organizations, specifically in appraising current performance, is essential to success. A more positive and productive way of looking at it is that at last the real importance of Quality has been realized, and thank goodness we are getting more help in managing it!

The reaction of some traditional Quality Control departments is understandable and leads to the next major difference between the traditional and new concepts. Typically in the past Quality has been perceived to be in competition with other pressures and priorities in the business, and invariably it has come off second best. Many organizations actually pay lip service to Quality. They say that it is vital, they make pronouncements about it, they pressurize employees to improve Quality, and yet when it comes down to it, so often it is quantity that rules the day. The actual behaviour of the organization says, 'get the product out of the door, we'll sort out the problems later'. People say 'do you want quantity or quality, make your mind up'. The new concept we are talking about here changes all of this. Quality is no longer a rather poor relation and neither is it in competition with other priorities; it becomes first amongst equals and, what is more, it becomes the major mechanism for achieving other goals, from productivity to cost savings, from staff morale to customer satisfaction. This is not going to happen simply because we say that it would be a rather nice idea; clearly there has to be a reason for it and the reasoning has to make commercial sense. This leads to the fourth major difference between traditional and new Quality.

In the past Quality has typically been 'controlled' via the Quality Control department, and the basic methodology for this has been to sample finished products and respond to the findings. If there were too many errors in the batch then the whole batch had to be rejected and reworked or scrapped, depending on the product. The Quality culture was an 'appraise and react' one. Looking at things this way round it is easy to see how the almost traditional competition between Quality and production came about. It is also easy to see how Quality was viewed as a relative thing to be put alongside other competing priorities. The logic was that it costs a lot of money to set up a system for assessing the Quality of finished products and even more for reworking Quality problems. Quality was viewed as being costly and problematical. Because of this it was considered only to be worthwhile aiming at improved Quality up to a point. The view was taken that there came a time when the costs involved in putting things right outweighed the benefit to be gained. Typically this was expressed graphically, as shown in Figure 1.

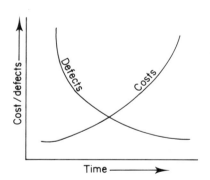

Figure 1. Appraise and react culture

There is not much wrong with the logic of this argument and frankly it has been, and still is, the way that most organizations manage Quality. This all changes rather dramatically with new Quality, however, because here we attack the question of Quality from a different end, by establishing that the 'appraise and react' method is not the only option, since presumably we could try to prevent things going wrong in the first place. If we invested in this, rather than in reacting to problems when they occurred, the economics might change somewhat.

In fact there are three types of cost which are directly associated with Quality. Two of these are costs of trying to get the work right first time. The first is the cost of the assessments and appraisals done by the Quality Control department and the second is anything we invest in trying to prevent things going wrong in the first place, things like training people properly, planning ahead, investing in tools, techniques, and technology which will help prevent failures occurring. The third type of cost is associated with getting it wrong the first time. Such things as rework, scrap, warranty costs, customer complaints departments, and ultimately lost customers through not meeting their requirements. Ask yourself, given the three types of cost—cost of failure, of appraisal, and of prevention—which you spend most on in your organization. Most companies spend a vast amount more on correcting failure than they do on anything else, often three or four times more than on prevention and twice as much as on appraisal.

The new Quality concept redirects the organization's investment in Quality by changing the 'appraise and react' culture to a 'prevent' culture. This is not only achieved by exhortation but by solid investment in prevention activities and mechanisms. Again this can be expressed on a graph as in Figure 2.

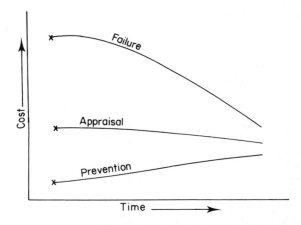

Figure 2.   Cost of Quality over time with the new Quality concept

By investing appropriately in prevention across the whole range of work that is done in the organization, the total cost of Quality can be reduced, and usually very significantly. At this point let us remind ourselves that new Quality does not only concern itself with production activities; all the work that is done in the organization by every employee is included. A typist having to retype a letter is a cost of failure just as much as a faulty component in a product, an invoice which has to be reworked is as well, and so is an expense claim form which has to be resubmitted and a management report which is not thorough enough and has to be done again.

By working on and investing in prevention we can effect a major reduction in the cost of failure. The cost of appraisal is important and can be maintained, and overall we come to a situation where the cold, hard economics of new Quality are that as we reduce the number of defects through prevention and therefore as we reduce our cost of failure, so does our total cost of Quality reduce, as shown in Figure 3. What is more all of these 'savings' go directly to improve the profitability of the organization.

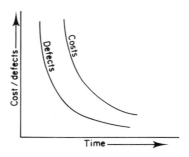

Figure 3.   Basis of prevent culture

The fourth main difference between traditional and new Quality is that in the past Quality has been viewed as an 'appraise and react' activity and this always led to the correct assumption, given this culture, that it was only economically viable to improve Quality up to a certain point. Today, with the focus heavily on prevention rather than cure it is a very different story, since in this scenario we can see that our cost of Quality and therefore our total organizational costs reduce as we make more and more improvements in Quality. We all know that to reduce costs adds directly to the 'bottom line' of the business without having to sell anything to a single extra customer, and that is why with new Quality prevention is the name of the game, not as something which is 'nice to do' but rather as a vital 'need to do' for solid commercial and financial reasons.

The fifth main difference stems out of this recognition. Most of us are brought up in a way that views Quality as a relative thing. We get 90 per cent in a school test and congratulate ourselves and go off to play a game in the playground. At work we get most things right and we see everyone else as the problem. If we are dealing with suppliers we give them some leeway in what they ship to us by imposing what are called acceptable quality levels (AQLs) on them. Typically an AQL says that an acceptable level of Quality for the supplies being purchased will be 95 or 98 per cent whatever number is deemed appropriate. It is accepted that 'people make mistakes', 'you can't win them all', and so on. Most of us have an acceptable quality level mentality. We ask ourselves whether it is worth it economically, or timewise, or in sweat to go for the remaining 5 or 2 per cent.

With new Quality the AQL mentality is replaced progressively by one which strives for completely defect-free performance in all work done by anyone in the organization. Before we dismiss such a preposterous idea as totally unworkable, let us remind ourselves that working on preventing defects actually reduces the total costs of the organization, and so is a 'profitable' activity in its own right. Harold Geneen of ITT once said that Quality was their most profitable product line!

We may also gain some strength and inspiration from two champions of industry, one from the East, the other from the West. Kanosuke Matsushita, President of Matsushita Corporation, once said: 'It is difficult, but we have to get rid of the idea that we can permit some leeway simply because total elimination of defects is so difficult.' Thomas J. Watson Sr., the former Chief Executive of IBM expressed the same viewpoint and put it in a beautifully succinct way when he said: 'It is better to aim at perfection and miss, than to aim at imperfection and hit.'

The message of new Quality is that we are embarked on a journey, a journey to defect-free, a journey that will never end. It is a profitable journey, and one that must involve all employees from the chief executive down. If anyone is not with us on the journey then we are simply giving people permission to make mistakes, and increasingly this does, and will continue to, undermine the viability of our business. No one is saying that we have to be perfect starting from tomorrow, since for most organizations this would mean ceasing trading! The point is that we are constantly, irrevocably, and in a controlled and organized way going down the road of fewer and fewer defects, the road leading to perfection.

In summary, what are the differences between the traditional and new Quality approaches? Firstly, the definition of Quality as 'meeting customer requirements now and in the future' implies measurement. This is the key, and more so now that Quality becomes a matter for all employees rather than just production people, because the customer is defined as the next person or people our work goes to, thus opening up the concept of the internal as well as the external customer. Thirdly, the old 'appraise and react' culture is replaced by one which invests in 'prevention', and does so because it recognizes that it makes commercial sense to do so. Fourthly, Quality, rather than being as it so often has been, the Cinderella, now emerges as the Princess, first amongst equals—not in competition with other priorities but helping and assisting them. Preventing rework, for example, increases productivity. Is it ever cheaper and better or faster to do it right the second time? Producing work which meets the requirements of our internal customers increases their own satisfaction and general morale. Doing it right first time reduces the costs of scrap, the savings from which go straight to the bottom line of our company results. Finally, because the aim is to get it right first time, for economic reasons, the old 'acceptable quality level' philosophy is replaced by one which seriously aims at working towards a defect-free environment in everything we do.

What will this all be worth? Why should we bother? If we ask the IBMs and ITTs of this world, they measure the benefits of the Quality process they have embarked on in billions of dollars. For smaller organizations we may need to take a couple of noughts off the end, but we are still talking about very substantial sums of money. In most organizations the cost of Quality under the traditional Quality banner runs at a minimum of 20 per cent of sales revenue, and often it is much higher than this—sometimes approaching 50 per cent of sales revenue. Even in this situation companies can be reasonably successful, and blissfully unaware of the potential that they have for improvement, since there is every reason to suppose that, through the pursuit of Excellence, with Quality as the main lever, this figure can be brought down to under 5 per cent in the long term. However, let us be really cautious and conservative. Let us assume that the cost of Quality is currently 20 per cent of sales and we can only get it down to 10 per cent. The cost reduction is 10 per cent of sales, and this goes as a straight contribution to profit before tax, without a single extra product or service having been sold, and most likely with a number of more satisfied customers than has been the case previously. And all because we did more things right the first time! In practice the figures are likely to be better than this over time, and any organization striving for Excellence in this way should easily pay for its investment in prevention year by year. There is no need to wait for years before reaping the benefits of our investment or labour; it will almost always be self-financing as we travel on the journey.

Chapter 11

THE QUALITY STRUCTURE

Any large-scale project or process requires organized coordination, and this is certainly the case on the Journey to Excellence. When dealing with organizational change we are dealing with something of enormous complexity. Clearly we do not wish to get bogged down in this, and there is therefore, from the outset, a need for a central coordinating body whose job it will be to steer the whole process and keep it on track. This will normally best be organized as a group. The main job of members of this group is to be able to see through the complexities involved and, using their knowledge of the concept, to be able to help other employees to do the same. Such groups will always work more effectively if they have some budgetary authority, and this should be built in to their remit if at all possible. Since the process of achieving 'Excellence through Quality' involves an active investment in measures to ensure the prevention of defects, as was outlined in the previous chapter, there is a budgetary aspect to the taken into account, and especially since the chief executive needs to be a member of the group, an appropriate vehicle for making such decisions will normally be the overall steering group. This group will be responsible for decisions about phasing and timing for the whole programme and is a key focal point for the whole process.

Key functions which form the core of the group's activities are:

To provide training, resources, and support for any Quality activities

To commission Quality activities as appropriate, specifically Quality task forces

To track progress being made by groups working on Quality activities

To recognize groups and individuals for their efforts and success on Quality work

To spread the word throughout the organization to demonstrate both personal and organizational commitment

To make the whole process enjoyable for everyone who joins in

This group can be called by any name, common ones being the Quality council, the Excellence steering committee, and the Quality steering group. More important, however, is the composition of the group, and here there are some clear guidelines which should be followed closely. Number one is that in companies where employees are represented by a trade union, officials of the union or unions should, of course, play a full part in the steering group. It is essential that the Journey to Excellence is, and is seen to be, a collaborative venture. Excellent companies both deserve and tend to have excellent industrial relations, and excellent industrial relations come out of fostering a full involvement of all parties in important issues to do with the future prosperity of the organization.

The second guideline is that the composition of the group should, as far as possible, reflect the structure of the company, with people from different divisions, functions, and levels playing a role. Thirdly, the chief executive must be a full member of the group. Without him such a body does not make any sense. Fourthly, the person appointed as the Quality director should be included in the group since he will have a lot of detailed and up-to-date information about activities to share with other members. The whole group should not number more than twelve people, and in smaller organizations the number can usefully be reduced to seven or eight.

With any steering committee there are ever-present dangers, firstly of becoming a self-perpetuating 'standing committee' which says much and achieves little. The Journey to Excellence is a process about getting things done, and it is essential that this group takes the lead in this respect. If it becomes an extension of the negotiating procedure, or a mechanism for personal glorification, it will not work, and it will endanger the whole process. Because the success of this group is so important it will be useful, at the outset at least, for it to have someone available to stand back from the work of the group and look at how the members are working together. This role can be given to one of the facilitators whose role is described later in this chapter or to the external consultant if one is being used.

As well as this main steering group, in an organization of any size it is likely to be necessary to have departmental or divisional quality councils to support the activities on a local basis. Whereas it is important not to bog down the process with bureaucracy, it is important in a positive way to have people who are constantly thinking about the future of the process and who are actually managing its success. As a rule of thumb there should be a separate Quality council for each work group, department, function, or division of more than about three hundred people.

These steering groups obviously need to have a clear understanding of the process of achieving Excellence through Quality and should also be trained in the problem-solving structure which will be used by the Quality teams to solve problems and exploit opportunities.

The second aspect of organization for Excellence through Quality concerns the staffing that is required. Any organization wishing to achieve Excellence through Quality will need to appoint someone to the job of Quality director. This will need to be a full time appointment for all but the smallest of companies, where a part time appointment will be adequate. Even in this latter situation, however, it will be essential that the responsibilities be reflected in both the job description and the salary for the job. Having an active and successful Quality director really is fundamental to the overall success of the process. It is equally important that everyone in the organization sees that it is a senior and well-respected person who has been given the job, rather than someone having been pushed sideways. Put in a nutshell, people have got to sit up when they hear the name of the person appointed and say, 'This must be important if they are giving the job to him!' This role will be a new one for organizations embarking on the journey and so a sample job description for the Quality director is given below.

Outline job description for Quality director

Overall job purpose

To ensure the success of the Excellence through Quality process in the organization in both the short and long term.

Key job functions

1. **To be actively involved in setting up Quality activities (QTFs, QDGs, QITs, QCs).**

2. **To sell the concept within the organization and progressively gain full and active commitment from all employees.**

3. **To arrange for and participate in the training and education of all employees in Quality concepts, processes, and activities, including facilitator training.**

4. **To manage other facilitators as they become necessary.**

5. **To facilitate Quality activities.**

6. **To maintain an effective internal marketing programme associated with Excellence through Quality.**

7. **To report progress on the progress being made in Excellence through Quality to the chief executive on a regular basis. The reports are to include quantified measurements.**

8. **To assist in the process of making the concept 'business as usual'.**

The right person to undertake this job will be someone with particular talents. An outline person specification is included below which may be useful in thinking through the type of person best suited for the job.

Outline person specification for Quality director

The person fulfilling the role of Quality director:

* **Must be able to deal really effectively at all levels of the organization.**

    Reason: **Reports to chief executive, needs to sell concept to all levels, will facilitate Quality Circles.**

* **Must be persuasive.**

    Reason: **A key job function is to sell the concept.**

* **Needs to be energetic and persistent.**

    Reason: **The selling part of the job is hard work and goes on for ever. There will always be someone who needs 'converting'.**

* **Needs to be a positive thinker.**

    Reason: **The process is not irrevocably positive. It often involves taking three steps forward and two steps backward. There will be sceptics and cynics.**

* **Needs to be imaginative.**

    Reason: **There is much scope for creativity in the job, for example with the internal marketing programme.**

* **Needs to be organized.**

    Reason: **Will be dealing with many different types of people at all levels in a wide variety of meetings. Will often be responsible for the 'secretarial' role. It is not envisaged that the job should carry a significant staff back-up.**

   The third aspect of the Quality structure which needs addressing is the requirement for people to assist the different types of group in the early stages of their work. These people are commonly known as facilitators. The facilitator role is utterly essential to this whole process and it is therefore extremely important that the right kind of people are selected and trained. The job of the facilitator is easy to describe, but less easy to do well. In essence it is to help the groups with which he is working to become self-sufficient as soon as possible. This instantly makes the job a rather unusual one in the sense that success is defined as not being needed any more. Since most people spend their working lives trying to make sure that they continue to be needed, clearly a rather distinctive type of person is required for this job.

The job of facilitating Quality groups and activities focuses on the process of work rather than the task itself. In other words, the facilitator is a trainer and developer of people and groups, someone who does not get too involved in the details of the problem, but concentrates on helping the groups to use the problem-solving process and the techniques successfully and on working together effectively. The facilitator attends group meetings for as long as is required for the group to be able to continue working successfully by itself. He also works with the leader of the group in preparing and reviewing the meetings, and continues to do this until the leader has developed in confidence and ability to the point of being able to run successful group meetings in his own right. The facilitator, it is important to note, does not own the groups he works with, and must make quite sure that this does not happen in practice.

Clearly training will be required to equip people for the facilitator role. This should focus on developing a range of skills including a thorough knowledge of the problem-solving process, the skills of developing individuals, an understanding of what happens in groups, and the requirement, in terms of training, for leaders and members of the different types of group which form the core of Quality activities. The kind of person who will be a good facilitator does not necessarily come from the training department of the organization; indeed he can come from any area. One strategy which works very well, especially in larger companies, is to make the job of facilitator a part of the manpower development process and to build in a spell of 1 to 1.5 years as facilitators for managers who are seen as having a bright future in the organization. People who have undertaken this role know how stretching it is, and also what a great deal of personal development there is in the job. This way of organizing things leads directly to a win/win situation, with the process itself gaining the use of good people as facilitators, which in turn helps the members and leaders of the groups, and the facilitators themselves gaining considerable experience in the process.

Clearly it would be best if the facilitators can be full time appointments since this will ensure that the required time and concentrated effort is being put into the different activities. It may be, however, that we need to use part time resources at the outset to ensure that the groups get sufficient back-up and support. Where this is the case, experience suggests that problems can occur, as the demands of the main-line job can make it very difficult for people, however committed, to continue to give the time that is required. Again, therefore, it would be better to organize the use of part time facilitators on what we could term a 'contract basis'. In effect this means that people who are keen will commit themselves to facilitating one or more groups, for a specified period of time, after which they can either terminate or renew their 'contract'. This may at first glance seem like an unnecessary piece of bureaucracy, but in practice it is not, for it helps to ensure that groups are not let down when they need support, whilst accepting that there are competing priorities that people have to live with. Furthermore, just as full time facilitators gain considerably in personal terms from the experience, so do part timers, and certainly the exposure to such activities in this role considerably helps their membership and leadership of groups that they are involved with. It is therefore entirely within the spirit and practice of Excellence to train a range of people as facilitators; indeed some of the major organizations have ongoing programmes to ensure a constant supply of trained and committed helpers.

There is no absolute rule as to the number of groups that a full time facilitator can handle, but experience indicates that given a range of new and 'mature' groups one person can handle twenty to thirty. At the outset when all of the activities are new, the number is much smaller, probably no more than about six groups, and it is obviously important not to attempt too much if this will endanger the level of support these groups require. In thinking about the requirement for facilitators it should be borne in mind that the Quality director should be a trained and active member of the team, especially at the start and with the first few groups.

The keys to the Quality structure are the steering committees, the Quality director, and the facilitators. As far as reporting relationships are concerned, the Quality director should report directly to the chief executive, although obviously a lot of the week to week reporting on progress will be done to the main steering committee. Full time facilitators will report to the Quality director and part time facilitators to the Quality director for this part of their work. This is another reason why it is important to establish a clear 'contract' for part timers.

Chapter 12

BASIC QUALITY EDUCATION

A core part of the process of achieving Excellence and Quality is the reeducation of all employees in the organization to an understanding of the concept. A key principle of the whole concept is that everyone has to be involved, and as such it is clearly essential that everyone knows what they are to be involved in. The training of staff is a requirement, in practice, which will be ongoing as the need and desire for learning more advanced and sophisticated facets of this concept develop. At the outset, however, it is a basic induction process that is required and, in reality, it will be necessary to construct two slightly different programmes to fulfil the need. The full model for achieving Excellence through Quality begins with the establishment of an organizational philosophy and a core mission statement. It continues with an audit of various basic organizational processes and the development of action plans to correct anything inappropriate that is found, or further to develop different aspects if necessary as indicated by the auditing process. The way this work is carried out involves the use of groups selected from appropriately skilled members of the organization. This work, generally speaking, precedes the introduction of the Quality concept to employees in general and it is therefore necessary for those who are actively involved at this stage to receive a full briefing. Furthermore, and since some non-management members of staff will be involved in this early work, it is necessary to fully brief all managers, so they are not surprised by any of the work being done and thus feel excluded or the victims of poor communication. The implication of all this is that there is an initial requirement for briefing sessions for management and others who are involved in the audit teams; these should be organized in groups of about twelve and in a 'top-down' fashion. The design of this programme would include consideration of, and discussion around, the full Excellence and Quality model, including the philosophy, mission, and 'the basics'.

There is a second requirement which is, ultimately, to induct every member of staff into an understanding of the new Quality concept. At this stage, there is no real reason to spend a lot of time contemplating the need for a philosophy, a core mission, and so on, since by then they will have been defined, but their importance needs to be emphasized, and the agreed outcomes of the philosophy and core mission meetings need to be shared with an appropriate emphasis on selling the benefits of having such clarifying statements. Furthermore, it will, in these sessions, suffice to establish that the audit of organizational basics has occurred or is in the process of being completed, and to clarify the kind of actions that are in hand to ensure an appropriate environment for Excellence and Quality to be achieved. The main focus of this second type of briefing meeting should, however, be the new Quality system which will affect everyone's working life from that time on. What follows is a detailed account of how to set up and run the first of these training sessions, together with a recommendation as to the content which should be included. The general session for all staff needs a different agenda, as indicated above, but many of the sessions will be the same. The sessions requiring a different structure are pointed out in the text.

Basic Quality education

Background

This course will be run for all management in the organization and also for any other member of staff who is involved in the initial audit groups. The programme lasts for a full day and is designed to blend formal inputs with an appropriate level of discussion to ensure understanding, to air differences of opinion, and to develop the early stages of ownership of the concept amongst participants. Specifically, it is designed to be run once the decision to introduce this process has been taken. It is therefore a 'selling' course only in the sense of trying to encourage interest, enthusiasm, and ownership amongst those attending; it is not designed to sell the concept into the organization in the first place.

It will always be sensible to name the concept so that people will be able to relate easily to it, and also to assist the marketing process. A soap powder without a name would not sell many packets—look at brand X! For this concept the title 'Excellence through Quality' is descriptive and appropriate in most organizations.

Administration

It is essential, for any course to succeed, that the administration and back-up is sound. For any programme that has the word 'Quality' in its title it is doubly so; therefore do pay attention to the detail. It is strange how some people will extract particular delight in pointing out a spelling error on a slide or a nameplate, a wrongly assembled handout, or a guest speaker who does not arrive on time. Merely by running Quality programmes, we stick our necks out, and so in administering the courses, look out for at least these points. There are other factors that can impinge, but these are the basics.

1. Arrangements for a senior manager, preferably the chief executive, to open the course.

2. One room large enough to hold the number attending in comfort, arranged in a 'horshoe' facing the trainer's materials.

3. An overhead projector, or slide projector depending on how the visual aids are presented.

4. A flip chart and pens.

5. Masking tape.

6. Spare projector bulbs.

7. Scribbling pads and pencils for participants.

8. Photocopies of training material as required.

9. Other handouts as required.

Session 1—Introduction (15 minutes)

This session is designed for the chief executive of the organization publicly to state his commitment to the concept of Excellence through Quality.

Session outline

The session should be structured round the following points, which should be expressed in individual words and style:

1. We are a changing organization in a changing world.

2. The world is becoming more selective and more conscious of value for money.

3. If we do not provide our products and services in a way which satisfies the requirements of our customers, they will find someone else to supply them that will.

4. We need to be even more conscious of Quality than we have ever been.

5. As such, we have decided to introduce, and maintain, a concept called Excellence through Quality which you are here to hear about today.

6. Do not think that this is a gimmick—this is survival.

7. This process has already changed me and the way I do things for the better, and it will continue to do so. I will be actively participating in the whole thing. It is *not*, repeat *not*, a case of 'do as I say, not as I do'. It is exciting, interesting, rewarding, and utterly essential for our survival—please listen carefully and join in the discussion.

8. I want to hand you over now to (internal trainer/external consultant) who will lead the discussion.

9. Thank you.

Session 2—An introduction to the programme (15 minutes)

This session is designed as a backcloth to why the subject of Excellence and Quality is important and as a statement of what expectations we should have in terms of such things as the time it is likely to take.

Session outline

Try to get some interaction going to loosen things up. If everyone says something, especially after the introductions, it will be good.

1. (Optional) Let's go round the room and introduce ourselves to each other, starting with me.

2. The administrative arrangements for our time together are as follows.

3. In the last few years, two words have really hit the headlines. The first is Quality, the second, Excellence.

4. Quality nowadays is almost synonymous with Japan, yet thirty years ago Japan produced little but junk.

5. Many organizations have tried and are trying to copy Japan, often with little success. This is because they are trying, but out of context. Rather like a transplant operation, many replacement parts will be rejected.

6. Since Peters and Waterman wrote *In Search of Excellence*, thousands of people have spoken millions of words on the subject. Many of these words have been elegant, but nonetheless, wish fantasies, without any real chance of becoming reality.

7. We, as an organization, are embarking on a long-term process which will help us to become, and to remain, truly Excellent. It will take a long time, indeed the process will go on for ever. There is no magic. There are no quick fixes. All the experts say that what we are about to embark on takes years not months.

8. This is a process which will touch every part of the organization and every person in it. No one will be excluded; everyone must play their part if we are to succeed.

9. It is not only interesting but is exciting and rewarding, as our chief executive has said.

Session 3—The company philosophy (15 minutes)

Here we are trying to pass over to the participants the vital importance of having a philosophy in the organization, the philosophy being the way we do things, as opposed to what we do. (This session will need to be redesigned for the staff programmes.)

Session outline

Make sure that people understand the difference between the way we want to do things and what we want to do.

1. Discuss what is a company philosophy.

2. Give examples of company philosophies, for example:

   Company A   —   Respect for the individual
                      Customer service
                      Excellence in everything we do

   Company B   —   Our company is our customer and our staff

   Company C   —   Respect for: (a) colleagues
                                   (b) clients
                                   (c) the organization

3. Discuss briefly what this company stands for at the moment.

4. Explain that a group will be working on the philosophy that will be adopted by the organization and communicated to everyone. (Note: If the group has already met and agreed the philosophy, it should be discussed in terms of

acceptability, believability, and commitment, and this should be added to the framework of the session and become a key part of the discussion.)

Session 4—The core mission (15 minutes)

The focus here is on what we do rather than how we achieve it. This session will need to be redesigned for the staff programmes.

Session outline

Reinforce the difference between the philosophy and the mission.

1. Discuss what is a core mission. It is the fundamental purpose of the organization expressed in a simple communicable way.

2. Discuss what people's perceptions are as to what the mission of this organization is currently, and because of the differences which emerge discuss how difficult it is to set one.

3. Establish that a group will be working the core mission and that it will be openly communicated to everyone. (Note: If the group has already met, adjust the session to discuss its work and the result.)

Session 5—The basics (30 minutes)

Excellence and Quality cannot be achieved in an organization without first getting the basics right. Here we introduce the key basics.

Session outline

Get a discussion going about the basics in this organization. Try to generate an interest in playing a part in investigating the basics.

1. Excellence and Quality depend on having the basics of the organization in good shape.

2. In this session we will go through key basics and discuss any extras you think should be included.

3. The key basics are:

   Organization structure
   Management

Communication
Customer orientation
Ownership

4. I would like to go through these in turn.

5. *Structure*. Organization structure is very important. There are no ultimate answers. The guidelines, however, indicate:

Small versus large
Decentralized versus centralized
Small staff functions versus large staff functions
Rotating staff personnel versus professional staff personnel
Close to the end customer versus distant from him.

6. *Management*. Any process of this kind can only be successful if it is really supported by management. Supervisors and managers, therefore, need to be the right people in the right place at the right time doing the right things using the right skills, so the key features here revolve round:

Selection
Appraisal
Counselling
Goal setting
Training
Development

7. *Communication*. Communication is obviously a truly key feature in any organization. Mechanisms are needed for:

Downward, e.g.	briefing groups
	department meetings
Upward, e.g.	suggestion schemes
	a system for appealing the line against unfair treatment
	opinion surveys
Lateral, e.g.	cross-functional projects
	rotation
	company meetings

8. *Customer orientation*. Organizations need to be sure that they focus on their customers. This sounds obvious but all too often is forgotten. Questions here include:

How customer orientated are our staff?

What differences are there between those dealing direct with the customer and others in terms of customer orientation?
Is there any notion of the 'internal customer'.

9. *Ownership*. Organizations need to make it worthwhile for employees to commit themselves. This can come in different forms:

Sharing the actual ownership of the organization
Creating a high performance, high reward payment structure
Psychological ownership—a feeling of being a valued part of the organization

Session 6—Auditing the basics (15 minutes)

This session is a description and discussion around the appropriate mechanisms and people for the audit process.

Session outline

1. The idea is to get groups together to audit the basics.

2. Given the topics to be 'audited', discuss who we want to involve in the auditing of the different subjects.

3. Remember, we want to involve staff, where appropriate, as well as management.

4. Discuss group size.

5. Discuss the amount of back-up the groups would be likely to need in the shape of consultants/facilitators.

Session 7—An introduction to Quality (30 minutes)

At this point we are ready to introduce the word Quality into the discussion. It is essential that those attending 'get the message' and also we want as many as possible to commit themselves to it.

Session outline

This session revolves round a discussion of the new meaning of the word Quality and its implications.

1. Invite definitions of the word Quality.

2. Discuss these and indicate that they tend to be expressed as generalizations,

e.g. 'good', 'high class', 'expensive', 'elegant'. Some definitions point to the broad idea of 'customer satisfaction'.

3. Point out that quality is often defined as 'customer satisfaction' and that the problem with this is that it is a vague and amorphous concept.

4. Ask how many people have felt the urge to write a letter of complaint and yet have not done it. Point out that as far as the offending company is concerned they have a satisfied customer. They have no tangible evidence to the contrary. This is often the problem—how many of us give feedback as often as we should?

5. Of course, it cannot be solely the customers' responsibility—the supplier has a vested interest in the matter.

6. What is the problem here? In a nutshell it is one of measurement.

7. Take a situation. We go to a restaurant with our partner, we have a meal, we leave either a small tip or no tip at all because we were not really satisfied, we leave quietly, we do not return to the same restaurant. Nothing particularly unusual here, but it is a strangely frustrating feeling because there was nothing dramatically wrong. Indeed, as far as the restaurant is concerned, we were satisfied customers—nothing was said or done to indicate otherwise.

8. What are the kind of things that could have influenced this feeling of dissatisfaction? List ideas on the flip chart. Include such possibilities as:

   Took a long while to show us to our table
   Seemed to take ages before our order was taken
   Second course arrived too soon after the first
   The steak was maybe a little overdone, but not enough to warrant sending it back
   Wine was not really served at the right temperature
   Had some difficulty attracting the waiter's attention

9. The problem we all have, customers and suppliers (us, the restaurant, the waiters, and so on), is that we are talking in generalities, for example:

   How long is 'a long while' or 'ages' or 'too soon'?
   What is 'a little overdone'?
   What temperature is right?
   How long does it take to have 'some difficulty' attracting the waiter's attention?

10. All of these judgements go to affect our level of satisfaction and this is the commonly used definition of quality. Thus we are often left in the bizarre situation of us, as customers, feeling that the quality of what we have received

was bad, and the supplier believing, quite sincerely, that it was good, because he has no specific information to the contrary.

11. How can we define quality in a more useful way? By making it more specific.

12. The new definition which we will use from now on is: 'Quality is meeting customer requirements, now and in the future.'

13. What is the difference? Let us go through the restaurant saga again and see. Involve the group in this. We go in—what was our first dissatisfaction? Maybe the delay in being shown to our table. What is our requirement? Specify it—within one minute, five minutes, what? When we decide this, and assuming we tell the restaurant or the waiter has asked us, we have a measure. We all know the customer's requirement and can work towards achieving it. What was the next problem? Maybe the delay before our order was taken? What is our requirement? Specify it. Go through a selection of the problems and reinforce the point about having stated and measurable requirements.

14. Establish that we now have mechanisms for measuring 'conformance to requirements' which we did not have before. Discuss how this can help both us and the restaurant. In a nutshell, we all know what we are dealing with and whether or not we have succeeded.

15. If participants raise questions and issues, discuss them. For example, 'It would be impossible to do this for every customer.' Discuss this. It may be difficult but actually not impossible to do some research and then to set performance standards, such as two minutes from entering the restaurant to sitting down. If we do not meet this then we can mark it down as a defect in the quality of our service.

16. Elicit examples from other situations where failure to set measurable standards can lead to the same frustrating result, for example the length of supermarket queues or the unavailability of stock. There are supermarket chains who look at the length of the queues and say, 'We must be doing well, what a quality organization we are!' Others say that if there are more than two customers waiting and there are empty checkouts, then we are not meeting our customers' requirements as far as speed of service is concerned. There are other examples from our own work areas, such as whenever somebody says 'as soon as possible' or 'I'll do it' but does not say by when. The examples are endless both at home and at work.

17. The second major difference with this definition is that the word 'customer' applies both to external and internal customers. Discuss what the concept of the internal customer means. It is the person we pass our work to. Discuss the implications of this concept. Establish that they are very wide and important.

Establish that they totally change the view we take concerning the work process internally.

18. Establish and specify that from now on the word customer will mean both the internal and external customer and that there should be no distinction between them. The idea is to 'meet customer requirements' whether they are internal or external customers.

19. The next step in achieving Quality, once we have met the customer's requirements: for now, is to be constantly on the search for improvements which will ensure that we meet his requirements in the future as well. Clearly this involves not only research on our part but also mechanisms for eliciting specific future requirements. Once we are ahead we will want to stay ahead.

20. In summary, Quality is meeting customer requirements now and in the future. Customer requirements, whether for internal or external customers, are precise and tangible things that need to be measured, and our performance in meeting them also needs tracking if we are genuinely to be in the business of supplying Quality goods and services.

Session 8—Implications of the traditional idea of Quality (30 minutes)

The purpose of this session is to look at the problems which stem from the traditional view of Quality.

Session outline

This part of the programme should be as much a discussion as is possible round the framework given.

1. The traditional view of Quality can lead to a range of problems. The restaurant owner thought he was giving a good quality service, yet he lost our custom. In other situations, major problems often emerge which have their roots in a failure to be specific in defining and meeting customer requirements. We need to look at how this happens.

2. One major problem with the traditional view of Quality is that it happens after the event. Typically a sample of what we produce is analysed for faults and then passed or rejected. In a service environment, a batch of customer complaints might trigger a 'purge' on Quality. The basic methodology is to 'control' Quality by appraising and reacting—hence, the Quality Control department. Can you think of examples of this appraisal and reaction in the organization? Are they all from the production area? Discuss how in a

traditional Quality environment Quality is often associated with the production area only. People often say, 'You can't apply it in our area—we don't make anything.' To what extent does this happen here?

3. Obviously it costs money to inspect, sort out the rejects, and then put things right. This leads to the second major problem with the traditional view of Quality, the belief that Quality is relative. If you put it on a graph it looks like Figure 1.

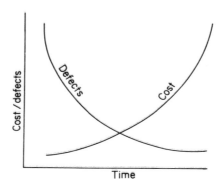

Figure 1

4. Looking at it like this the implication is that after a while it is not economically viable to continue trying to reduce defects (instances of not meeting customer requirements) since the benefit of doing so is outweighed by the cost. Thus Quality becomes a relative matter, in conflict with other priorities. How often do we hear things like 'Make your mind up, you can't have Quality and productivity!' Because Quality is assumed to be relative, standards are set, in the production area at least, in terms of acceptable quality levels, usually known as AQLs. The idea here is that we need to find the optimum quality level at which Quality is as good as can be achieved against the economic 'realities' of Figure 1. As such we target our suppliers at AQLs of 95 or 98 per cent defect-free supplies and accept the remaining faults. In non-product areas there are often no standards set and so we are in an even more difficult situation.

5. Elicit whether people see AQLs, or no standards, as a normal and acceptable practice? Agree that certainly it is normal.

6. Most of us organize our lives around the principle of the acceptable quality level. We get eight out of ten in a school test, pat ourselves on the back, and think of something else. At work we deal with batches of widgets or

paper; we get our part of the operation right most of the time, maybe even 99 per cent of the time, we pat ourselves on the back, and think of something else. We even have sayings to reinforce this notion. 'You win some, you lose some', and with a shrug of the shoulders we move on to the next thing. 'To err is human, to forgive divine', 'You can't win them all', and so on.

7. The problem is that if everyone is working at the same level of 99 per cent defect free, the cumulative effect of 1 per cent of errors is frightening. If it takes 500 components to make a product or service, and every component or ingredient is produced at the level of 99 per cent defect free, statistically 99.3 per cent of the end products or services will have defects in them! Staggering but true.

8. The third problem with the traditional view of Quality are the results. Often, of course, the results are perfectly satisfactory. In some ways, this presents a difficulty because it can hide the real dangers of this traditional view. Elicit examples of Quality problems from the organization. Try to relate these to the traditional view. One result is that Quality is always in competition with other aspects of the business, for example production. Even the sales force who want the Quality also want the output. Can anyone think of other examples?

Session 9—Quality: The new view (45 minutes)

Here we reinforce different aspects of the new view of Quality.

Session outline

Try to get discussion going to check understanding and acceptance of the new Quality concept.

1. If we meet the requirements of our customers we should get their buiness. If we meet their requirements now, and also focus on making sure that this remains the case in the future, we should retain the business. We have discussed the need for these requirements to be specified and measured, so that we have a mechanism for tracking performance.

2. With the new Quality concept, we can say that if it is not measured, it is not Quality.

3. One key difference with this new concept is the recognition that once it has happened, it is too late. Once my steak has arrived overcooked, it is too late to do anything about that steak. The only options are to send it back and spoil the meal for myself and any dining companions I may have, or

to accept what I do not really want to accept: either way it would have been cheaper and better to get it right the first time. Can anyone think of an example where it would be cheaper and better to get it right the second time? There aren't any. Therefore the whole focus of this new concept is on prevention rather than cure, on getting things right the first time.

4. Furthermore, this is not just a production line concept—it affects every single piece of work which is done in the organization. New Quality is for everyone in the organization; no one can be left out. Discuss this with the group.

5. The next major difference is that Quality now is not a relative affair competing with other priorities. Quality as of now becomes the first amongst equals, the Princess not the Cinderella. This is more than just fine words; it summarizes an economic reality. Remember the graph of traditional quality (Figure 1). With the new view and its focus on prevention, the whole situation changes to the one shown in Figure 2.

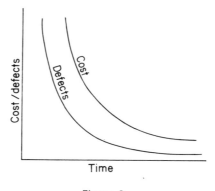

Figure 2

If we invest in Quality wisely, in other words in prevention, we can actually save money as the defects go down. Organizations that have established Quality programmes and have made Quality first amongst equals, companies such as IBM and ITT, recognize that Quality is not only a fine idea but also adds a great deal to their overall company performance. This is what we intend to do. The point with these new concepts is that they tell us that it is always worth working on preventing defects in our performance, not only because it is nice to do, but because it will actually improve our organization's performance.

This applies whether we are currently performing at a level of 90, 99 or even 99.9 per cent defect-free work; it is always worth investing time, energy, and money in preventing the remaining defects and thereby being more

95

successful in meeting the requirements of the customer. In other words, it is worth going for perfection in meeting the requirements of our customers or being, as we will call it, 'defect free'. How do you feel about this? Discuss it.

Explain that we are not saying that as of tomorrow everything will be defect free. This is a journey. A journey that will never end, but a journey that will make us Excellent. Share with the group the following quotes:

'It is difficult but we have to get rid of the idea that we can permit some leeway simply because total elimination of defects is so difficult.'
Konosuke Matsushita, President of the Matsushita Corporation
'It is better to aim at perfection and miss than to aim at imperfection and hit.'
T.J.Watson Sr.

6. The third key difference between new and traditional Quality is in the results. Put simply, increased profits without having to increase sales. How will it happen? This new concept means no trade-offs, no excuses, absolute clarity of the requirement for every member of staff to play an active role. In this way there should be no expensive surprises or things emerging from the woodwork; our customers internal and external will be satisfied because we will be specifying and meeting their requirements as we track our own journey to defect free.

7. Let us summarize the differences between traditional and new Quality. Try to involve the group in doing this.
   (a) Traditional Quality tends to be a vague and unspecific aim towards customer satisfaction. New Quality is specific, it is defined as meeting customer requirements, now and in the future. The requirements are specified beforehand.
   (b) Traditional Quality tends to be production orientated and relative. Quality rarely comes out top in a discussion about priorities; lip service is often paid to it. New Quality is first amongst equals. Not in competition any more, Quality pulls along productivity, profit, morale, and customer satisfaction. It is an organization-wide concept with everyone involved in it.
   (c) Traditional Quality gives permission to make mistakes through the acceptable quality level philosophy. New Quality takes us on a journey to defect-free performance in everything we do.
   (d) Traditional Quality is based on an appraise/react culture, so focuses on putting things right when they have gone wrong. New Quality switches the emphasis to prevention, so that we get it right the first time.
   (e) Traditonal Quality says that investment in Quality is only worthwhile up to a point. New Quality says that effective investment in prevention reduces the overall costs of the organization, and so it is always worth going for improvement in meeting customer requirements.

Session 10—Cost of Quality (30 minutes)

Here we introduce the idea of a mechanism for tracing our performance in achieving Excellence through Quality.

Session outline

The Cost of Quality is an important aspect of the whole Excellence through Quality process. It is therefore necessary for people to understand it. Furthermore, this session can help to reinforce some aspects of the new Quality philosophy, notably the idea of changing the balance of the investment in Quality from reaction to prevention.

1. One thing we need to help us on our Journey to Excellence is a tracking mechanism, since we have already said that if it is not measured, it is not Quality.

2. The mechanism we will use is called the Cost of Quality.

3. The total amount of time and money that we spend on Quality is the Cost of Quality. It is made up of different types of cost. Go through, clarify, and check understanding of them. They are:

    Cost of prevention. This is the cost of activities undertaken to prevent defects occurring. Examples include training in quality concepts, planning, potential problem analysis, buying machines which will help to prevent errors and defects.

    Cost of appraisal. These are the costs incurred while undertaking the normal work of the organization. Examples include Quality audits, inspection, control procedures.

    Cost of failure. These are the costs of getting it wrong the first time. Examples include rework in any part of the organization, customer complaints, having to pay extra because work was not scheduled accurately.

    Reinforce the three types of cost. Two are costs aimed at trying to meet the requirements of the customer. These are:

    Cost of prevention

    Cost of appraisal

    One is a cost of failing to meet the requirements of the customer. This is:

    Cost of failure

4. Elicit estimates from the group as to what proportion of the whole Cost of Quality is spent on each of the three. Usually it is heavily geared to cost of failure (say $\times$ 4) with cost of appraisal second (say $\times$ 2) plus cost of prevention last (say $\times$ 1).

97

5. Elicit estimates on what proportion of the organization sales revenue is spent on Cost of Quality in total. This will usually be in the order of 20 per cent of sales revenue, and could be as high as 50 per cent in some companies.

6. Establish that we will measure the current Cost of Quality in the organization and that we will continue to do so periodically as a measure of our progress.

7. Currently, we have agreed that the picture looks something like this. Draw a graph on the flip chart.

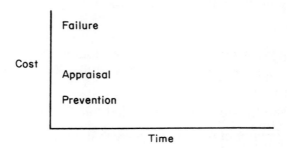

8. Establish that the aim in the future is to redistribute the Cost of Quality. Add to the graph.

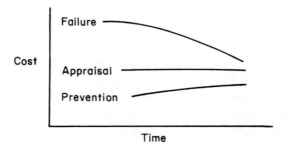

We want to reduce the cost of failure massively, keep the cost of appraisal about the same, and invest in prevention.

9. We intend to reduce the overall Cost of Quality significantly. This will improve our results without having to sell any more products or services. Harold Geneen of ITT once said that Quality was ITT's most profitable product, and what is more it was free! By measuring our Cost of Quality regularly we will

have an idea of how we are doing in our quest for achieving Excellence through Quality.

10. Establish that we need various things to help with this job:
    (a) Some rules of the game
    (b) A structure to work within
    (c) Techniques for doing it
    (d) The involvement of everyone who works here
    (e) Long-term commitment from management (last but most important)
    We will go through these in turn.

Session 11—The rules of the game: Basic Quality concepts (30 minutes)

Here we introduce the Quality concepts that the approach is based on; everyone in the organization needs to know them.

Session outline

Introduce the concepts one by one and discuss them with the group in terms of usefulness and believability.

1. We need some ground rules and basic concepts to act as a framework for this approach. In practice there are five of them. Write them up on the flip chart as you come to them.

2. The first is that this is a process rather than a programme. In other words, it has no end. Excellence through Quality is achieved in the process of trying to achieve it. Give the group the following puzzle. A frog is on a lily pad in the middle of a pool 2 metres in diameter. He wants to get out of the pool. He can jump half the remaining distance to the edge of the pool with each leap. How many jumps does it take him to get out of the pond?
    The answer is that he never gets out because he always has half the remaining distance to go. Help the group to see this if necessary. The point of the story is that this process is the same—it never ends. We get better and better, nearer the end result, but we always have some way to go. Discuss what is necessary to sustain the process. Listen to the responses of participants very carefully; there may be clues here for the internal marketing programme.

3. The second Quality concept is that Excellence through Quality stems from management action. Management must be behind it and actively involved in it for us to stand any chance of success. Everyone else in the organization plays a vital role as well, but the process is driven by management commitment and management action.

99

4. The third Quality concept is that to achieve Excellence through Quality every-one in the organization must be involved. If anyone is excluded, or chooses to exclude themselves, problems and defects are built into the system. What we need is a concerted effort to involve everyone. This does not mean that we all need to be involved in the same way—there are many different mechan-isms through which people can demonstrate their involvement, there will be a wide range of individual choices, and many of the mechanisms are voluntary. It will be required ultimately, however, that everyone is involved in one way or another. Discuss the practicability of this. Stress the long-term nature of the approach; we are not talking about everyone being involved starting tomorrow.

5. The fourth Quality concept is that we are embarking on a journey to defect-free performance in everything we do. This sounds like an impossible dream, but remember the two quotes we looked at earlier. Repeat the Matsushita and Watson quotes from Session 9. Another quote that is worth passing on is from John Opel, until recently Chief Executive of IBM. He said, 'If we do not provide the goods defect free the customer will find someone who will.' Providing defect-free goods and services means that we first have to specify with the customer, internal or external, what his requirements are; then we have to define how we will measure our performance in fulfilling the require-ments defect free. We all need to reorientate our thinking to take this new concept on board. Most of us think in terms of acceptable quality levels rather than this new concept, so we need to help each other understand it and live it.

   Remember as well we are not saying that everything has to be perfect starting from tomorrow. This is a real world concept. We are involved in a journey to defect free, a journey where we will set ourselves targets, measure our success, achieve results, pat ourselves on the back, and then set new targets that will take us further on the journey, measure our performance, and so on. We will be doing this as individuals and as teams and what is more we will all be trained in how to achieve it in an organized and systematic way, and we will be given the tools to do the job. Discuss this whole idea with the group and try to pass over a sense of excitement of going for defect free.

6. The fifth Quality concept is that appropriate investment in Quality reduces the total costs of the organization. In practice this means that we will invest in prevention and reduce the cost of failure, ultimately to zero. Do not let us think, however, that there is an immediate bottomless pit of money avail-able; again we have to live in the real world. Equally let us be very clear that we actively want to invest in prevention if it will stop failure. Amongst the techniques you will be taught will be how to make a case to the appro-priate level of management for spending money. Point out to the group that it

is a genuine belief that if we invest in Quality sensibly we will make more profit because our overall costs will reduce. Give examples from the particular environment of how reducing failure through preventive investment would reduce cost and increase profit. Make the point that increased profit secures our future and gives a bigger pot to be shared.

7. Summarize all five core Quality concepts, reinforcing their importance as you go through them.

Session 12—The basic structure of Excellence through Quality (45 minutes)

Here we outline the basic steps of the whole process and discuss them with participants.

Session outline

Try to generate a discussion around the key action steps—notably the 'putting our own house in order' and 'the bits between the boxes'.

1. The main steps of Excellence through Quality include all of the topics we have already discussed. Review these and then go through the remaining stages.

2. Stage 1 is to define the philosophy and then the core mission of the organization to give everyone guidelines for their behaviour and a clear 'tie-breaker' for making decisions.

3. The next step is to identify and to audit the key dimensions of the business. These should include:
   Organization structure
   Management
   Communication
   Customer orientation
   Ownership
   The way this is done is by setting up 'audit teams' containing interested and skilled people from within the organization.

4. Stage 3 is to hold training seminars for management and staff to induct them in the basic concept of new quality. This is one of these meetings. Everyone in the organization will be inducted in a similar way.

5. Stage 4 is to begin to give training in customer orientation and skills.

6. Stage 5 involves a detailed examination of what happens in each department currently, together with an assessment of the Cost of Quality, which will become the measure of our progress.

7. Stage 6 is to work on putting our own department's house in order, both as individuals and in teams. Discuss this. Reinforce the importance of doing this before Stage 7—otherwise all we will get is finger pointing.

8. Stage 7 is to analyse cross-departmental work processes in detail.

9. Stage 8 is to work on ridding these processes of defects again, both individually and in teams. Stress that this will not happen for a considerable while and that when it does it should not involve finger pointing between departments. Some of these stages are repeated and go on for ever, notably the Cost of Quality analysis will be repeated regularly to measure our progress. Also the activities involved in 'putting our own house in order' and working on 'the bits between the boxes' are ongoing. This reflects the fact that we are involved in a process rather than a programme.

Session 13—The main techniques for getting things done

Here we talk the participants through the four main types of group which will undertake much of the work. This is not a detailed introduction—that comes later when we are ready to set up the groups—but it will serve as an overview.

Session outline

Present the outline of the different types of group. Try to generate interest in them, but be careful that people do not immediately want to start on the cross-functional issues—that comes later.

1. Suggest that things will not just happen; we need to make them happen.

2. Say that there are tried and tested mechanisms which can help us and that we want to go through them in outline now. There will be detailed briefings later as we come to set up the activities.

3. Emphasize that we will not achieve Excellence through Quality without everyone's active efforts and that these mechanisms enable us to work at it together.

4. Point out that these mechanisms sound simple and in many ways they are, but they do require the use of an organized problem-solving structure which people who join in will be taught.

5. The first two types of group are called Quality Task Forces (QTFs) and Quality Department Groups (QDGs). Talk through the main characteristics as follows:
   Set up and 'owned' by management.
   Not voluntary.
   Deal with one issue selected by management then disband.
   Two to ten members are chosen for their knowledge of the subject.
   QTFs are usually cross-functional; QDGs are from one department.

Members can come from any level of the organization.
Meetings held as required.

6. The third groups are Quality Circles (QCs). The main characteristics here are:
   Entirely voluntary.
   'Owned' by the members of the group who select the issues to be worked on.
   Four to ten members, led by the supervisor in the first instance.
   Members are staff from a natural work group.
   Group is ongoing and aims at solving problems within its control and ulti-
   mately at achieving a Quality defect-free service to its customers.
   Meet one hour a week.

7. The fourth mechanism is Quality Improvement Teams (QITs). The main charac-
   teristics of QITs are:
   Voluntary.
   Owned by members.
   Leader and members come from anywhere in the organization.
   Subject based. People join a group if the subject interests them.
   Group can be started by anyone with an interest in a problem or topic.
   Two to ten members.
   Group lasts as long as there is interest and value in the subject.
   Meetings held up to one hour a week unless special authorization is
   received to increase the frequency.

8. Elicit views about the composition of the groups. Discuss the voluntary nature
   of Quality Circles and Quality Improvement Teams and establish the importance of this aspect.

Session 14—Management commitment (30 minutes)

This session is intended to elicit the support and commitment of management. An
alternative structure would be needed for the staff seminars, where the discussion
would be more about the believability of management commitment and the need
for staff to give managers the chance to show their commitment and their support.

Session outline

This session needs to be run as a free-flowing discussion. It is likely that some people
will be sceptical, some even cynical, but do not be deterred! This is normal and
understandable. There will also be some who are very enthusiastic.

1. State clearly that Excellence can only really be achieved through management
   actions. The whole process depends on this since 80 per cent of the things
   required to achieve Excellence are in management hands.

2. Therefore we all need not only to understand Excellence through Quality but also to commit ourselves to it and to play our part in the activities which are an integral part of it.

3. We have heard now about the whole approach, and we have had a chance to discuss it.

4. What are your reactions? What problems do you forsee? What benefits do you predict? Lead a discussion on people's reactions. Understand anyone's scepticism, but also express hope that this will turn to enthusiasm in time since the approach is here to stay. Reinforce the commitment of top management.

5. Share any further details of the plan as required. Try to achieve a desire for involvement.

Session 15—Wrap up (15 minutes)

The aim here is to let people know the timing of the next steps and to close the meeting on a high note.

Session outline

Try to assess the level of interest that the whole programme has generated.

1. Review with the group the next few stages of the work and the timing.

2. If appropriate, elicit the level of interest in being part of one of the audit teams.

3. Reinforce the message from the chief executive.

4. Reinforce that there is something in this for everyone and that we need everyone to play their part.

5. Reinforce that this is not a programme which will fizzle out. The Journey to Excellence through Quality is the journey of the future and goes on for ever.

6. Thank people for their attendance and involvement.

7. Ask for any final questions or comments. Close the meeting.

Chapter 13

MEETING CUSTOMER REQUIREMENTS

One of the major changes which is brought about during the Journey to Excellence concerns the perception people have regarding the word 'customer'. Almost universally the word is taken to mean the end user of the goods or services being offered. The practical effect of this is often damaging to the overall image and the performance of the organization. This comes about because most people in the company do not have a direct link with the customer, and usually see him as a pretty distant figure who does not really impinge on their lives in a day to day sense. In its turn this can often result in taking off the pressure that a direct interface with the customer brings, and can lead to defects and what we have called the 'acceptable quality level' mentality earlier in the book. This is the state of mind which says that a few defects here and there are both understandable as a part of human nature and acceptable in a business sense. As we now know, neither is the case for any organization seriously engaged in the Journey to Excellence, but such instances represent the reality in by far the majority of organizations up and down the land.

With the introduction of the Excellence through Quality process the word customer loses this exclusive focus on the outside, and becomes simply the word which describes who our work goes to, whether it be within the organization or outside it. Everyone who does a job as part of the organization receives inputs from one or more people, people henceforth called our suppliers. The job holder then adds value to these inputs in some way, before passing them on to his customers, who are the next in the chain. Any customer, whether internal or external, is as important as the next. This is a central and essential law of Excellence and must be engrained into every single employee's attitude and behaviour. It will not be easy, it will take a long time to achieve, but it is a key part of the process.

Along with the changed perception regarding the word customer, the second major change that is required in most organizations concerns the attitudes and behaviour of staff both to the end user and now to their internal customers. Generally speaking, people in organizations do not deal with customers particularly successfully. All of us can easily recollect occurrences when we felt we were not treated well as customers. It is all too regular an occurrence.

The training in meeting customer requirements, which is essential for every member of staff, usually requires either a one or two day course at the outset. It includes firstly a number of topics to do with our own state of mind, and secondly those aspects concerning the skills with which we deal with customers. The basic key to successfully orientating people to the customer lies in the first series of topics; in other words, it is largely to do with the state of mind people adopt in dealing with customers. The key dimensions of this training are dealt with in the following paragraphs.

For people to understand customers and deal successfully with them, the first essential recognition concerns perceptions. In dealing with people it is fruitless and counterproductive to become obsessed with what we consider to be the facts. It is a perhaps unfortunate reality that these are totally irrelevant compared to what the customer perceives, however wrongly in our view. We live in a world where people's perceptions guide their behaviour, and we are not different ourselves. As such it is vital that staff understand the subject of perceptions. There are many examples of how things can be interpreted differently by different people. Two 'classics' are the picture of the lady who to some appears to be an old hag and yet to others a beautiful young girl, and the picture which to some is the silhouette of two faces looking at each other and yet to others is an ornate vase. In both cases there is no trick involved, people look at exactly the same 'facts' and yet they see things differently. They have different perceptions. We know that the same happens all the time in everyday life. People apparently hear and see the same things and yet come to radically different conclusions, and stick to them through thick and thin. Such is the strength of this human phenomenon that we will be wise to assume in our behaviour that there are no facts, only perceptions. It sounds strange but it is a key basis for good customer relations, since it will help to avoid our slipping into dangerous and counterproductive win/lose arguments. The point which we need to get across to all employees here is that people talk about what they perceive to be right and it will not pay us to argue the rights and wrongs of their perception. We need to listen very carefully to what is being said and to try very hard to put ourselves in the position of the customer.

The subject of win/lose is the second important element for employees to be trained in understanding. Much of our culture is based on win/lose situations since, although we recognize cooperative effort and collaboration, we tend to emphasize 'healthy' competition. Clearly this attitude is right and proper in many cases, but there is a tendency for it to infiltrate into areas where it is not appropriate. Consider just a few such situations; for example any competitive sporting event is, by definition, a win/lose contest. This is perfectly right and proper, since there would be little point in playing many games unless there were the added 'spice' of competition. Equally it is entirely appropriate that organizations compete with each other to sell their goods and services, since this usually guarantees a better overall deal for the end users. There are many more such examples which could be discussed, but the point here is that all too often there is a tendency for win/lose to infiltrate into areas where it is not appropriate. Consider a fairly typical committee meeting. Members of the committee often interrupt each other to introduce their own ideas, proposals are made which are not even acknowledged and are therefore lost as the battle for members to 'win' with their own ideas continues. Often two or three members, recognizing strength in numbers, form a power block to support one idea against another; and some members appear to be planning their own counterarguments to points being raised, rather than listening to what is being said. These are all examples of individuals competing rather than collaborating as a group, and it is not that they are from competing organizations—far from it, they all work for the same company. Very often the original purpose of a committee is completely overshadowed by the development of these win/lose situations. This phenomenon does not only occur in committee or other group meetings, the organization is often affected by unhealthy win/lose situations in a far wider context. Typical examples of these would be office politics, interdepartmental arguments, and management/worker conflicts. In some organizations internal win/lose rivalries such as these appear to take up more time and effort than is devoted to the main product or service. It is almost as if people are trying to assist the outside competition by competing internally. Win/lose also happens very frequently in dealing with the end customer, especially in organizations which have not introduced the new Quality philosophy, with its insistence on stated and measurable requirements being the key to the relationship between supplier and customer. Even with the new 'rules of the game', however, there is a danger that staff try to 'beat' the customer by proving him wrong, or try to protect themselves by proving themselves right. Consider how many times in the average month we are told, in effect, that we are 'wrong' as end customers, that we do not understand the problem, that our complaint was unfounded, or that the product really did work—it was us that broke it!

There are obviously instances when win/lose is a positive factor, such as those dealt with earlier, but it too often leads to the poisoning of interpersonal relations and the reduction of the effectiveness of the organization. If a man loses an argument with his wife, he will often retaliate by being sullen and uncooperative, thus turning the win/lose situation into a lose/lose one.

This is the real problem—that win/lose rarely ends in this way. It so often continues with one form or another of revenge; for example, if an end user feels that he has 'lost', he can take his business elsewhere, thus reducing the business performance of the organization in question, and even internal customers can make life unpleasant and ineffective for suppliers who they perceive have put them in a losing position.

The situation we should be aiming at when dealing with our internal and external customers is one where everyone wins, and in dealing with our customers we have a primary responsibility to work towards this result. It is our job.

The skills required to enable staff to be successful in this should form part of the training given and include, firstly, developing the ability to listen actively and carefully to what is being said by the other person, rather than working out our counterarguments while he is speaking. To listen actively is one of the most difficult things to do well, and we can all improve our skills significantly in this. One problem here is that most people, in their heart of hearts, believe that they listen well and that it is others that have the problem. It really is important to develop this aspect of the training and the course should dwell on it. There are a wide range of practical exercises that can be used in the training environment, not only to highlight this aspect but also to give practice at improving our ability in it. The acid tests in listening actively are really hearing what the other person has to say, trying his reasoning on for size, and maybe also taking the risk of being persuaded. He is right in his own eyes, and he may end up being right in ours as well, if we actively listen to what he has to say.

The second skill in this area is not to make absolute statements which leave no room for modification, since these tend to polarize issues into win/lose terms. If someone says, 'that's the price take it or leave it, I don't care' or 'there is no way I will agree to that', the feeling that most people get is one of competition, win/lose, rather than the more productive feeling in a supplier/customer situation of both parties having gained something worth while. This requires training, of course, and also a change in the state of mind of many people since most of us tend to think in black and white terms and to be very evaluative. It will be much more productive when dealing with customers if we are able to avoid dogmatic statements which tend to cut off discussion and therefore our ability to identify and meet customer requirements. There are few, if any, questions or problems which cannot be viewed from more than one viewpoint and in our role as suppliers it is our responsibility not to stick immoveably to our own at the expense of hearing other possibilities.

None of this means, of course, that we have to end up agreeing with the other party, or even giving in to demands which we consider to be unwarranted. When the new concept of Quality is embedded it will be a rare occurrence indeed that customers and suppliers will have real differences since the requirements of the customer will have been specified in a quantified way, and measures will have been put in place to track progress in meeting them.

The third area of skill in dealing with customers concerns the detection of win/lose, since it can develop subtly. If we feel under attack or find ourself lining up our counterarguments while he is still talking then we are probably in a win/lose situation and have to be very careful not to promote it by our behaviour. It is so easy to respond to an apparent attack with, 'you should have known you weren't covered for that' or 'having it like that isn't going to do you much good, is it?' or 'but anyone with any sense would have seen that it wasn't right'. The examples are legion and they are heard every day.

We humans tend to be very competitive animals, and win/lose is the inevitable outcome of this. It is of course perfectly appropriate for us to compete with other suppliers for goods and services, just as much as it is appropriate for sports teams to go out and try to beat the opposition, as we have said before. What we are saying here, however, is that there are also areas where it is very counterproductive to compete, and that one of these is in dealing with our customers, both internal and external. One of the key ways of assisting this process, which should also be discussed in the training course devoted to developing skills in dealing with customers, is the basic definition and rule of the new Quality philosophy—that Quality is meeting stated customer requirements, now and in the future. Thus if we have met with the customer and established his requirements in a measurable way, we are halfway to being able to avoid win/lose, since we have the criteria in front of us both which define win/win.

It is, of course, easier to talk about keeping our dealings on a win/win basis than it is to do it in practice, and to a large degree our ability to do so depends on how 'healthy' we are as individuals. 'Unhealthy' people in a psychological sense tend to be very defensive and have a very limited ability to see sense in anyone else's view if it does not coincide with their own. They perceive themselves to be under threat, either actually or potentially, for much of the time and this tends to dominate their perspective and their behaviour. Because there are very few, if any, entirely healthy people, there is a serious need when engaged in the training of employees to discuss the subject and explore the things that are likely to happen if we do not feel comfortable in ourselves. This applies not only to what we are doing but also to who we are. Training of this sort, however, should certainly not be designed to be a crash course in humanistic psychology, neither should its focus be dominated by pure theory. Whatever is taught and discussed needs to be usable in a day to day sense. Fortunately this does not prevent us from using some of the profoundly useful work that has been done in the last few decades on the subject of understanding and developing psychologically healthy human beings. The reason for this is that some of the most interesting work that has gone on in this field in recent years has deliberately gone out of its way to make the findings useful and usable for the average man in a day to day sense. Perhaps the prime example of this is the model developed in the 1950s by Eric Berne and called 'transactional analysis'.

Transactional analysis (TA) claims to be the simplest and most effective method for not only understanding human behaviour but also helping to modify it. It is designed so that the layman will be able to understand and use it with relatively little training and without needing the ongoing help of psychologists or other experts. It is also designed to be safe in the sense that it does not require people to delve deeply into themselves unless they want to. This book is not intended to be a text on TA, and if the concepts which form TA are to be used in training staff in customer orientation there will be a requirement for further research or, preferably, the use of consultants with knowledge and skills on the subject. Having said this, it will be useful to give an overview of the core concepts which comprise this exciting approach since they should form part of the training given to staff in one format or another.

The basic assumptions of TA are firstly that people tend to learn ways of feeling and behaving at an early age and that these tend to become habitual regardless of whether they are appropriate any more. The second assumption is that it is feelings that cause us to behave in the way that we do. The third and key point is that we can control both our feelings and behaviour and change them for the better if we want to. The fourth assumption made by the approach is that we can all help each other in this quest for more appropriate behaviour. Finally, it is stated that feelings of doubt, indecision, embarrassment, fear, and anger are very counterproductive and cost organizations heavily in terms of time, money, and customer satisfaction.

The basic TA contention is that we can analyse what goes on between people in a simple, usable way. The 'transactions', as they are called, are analysed in terms of the three main modes of behaviour which are used by everyone in differing degrees. The three categories of behaviour are called 'parent', which is as it sounds, and includes both the 'critical' and the 'nurturing' roles, 'adult', which includes the cool, anlytical thinking type of behaviour, and finally 'child', which includes the free and spontaneous 'natural' child as well as the toned-down 'adapted' child who is more concerned with the acceptability of his behaviour to others. We all have all of these 'ego-states' and we use all of the behaviours, although in very different ways and patterns. TA helps us to analyse in a simple way what happens in a particular dialogue so that we can better understand why the outcome was as it was. Ultimately and with practice we can structure discussions so that healthy, win/win outcomes are much more likely. In a practical sense we can train people to understand what is really happening during a phone conversation with an irate customer and, more importantly, how to behave in an appropriate way which will defuse the situation and assist in reaching an acceptable solution for both parties. This situation happens frequently, of course, and often staff are able to deal with it very effectively, if intuitively. With this training employees should remain free to use their intuition, but will also have the knowledge to understand why and how some things work and others not. The success rate in these interactions increases dramatically when people understand what is really happening.

The second basic concept is based on the assumption that our habitual ways of feeling and behaving largely stem from the way we feel about ourselves in relation to others. These assumptions are called life positions because they tend to dictate what we do during our lives. Although most people remain in one or other of the four basic positions for much of the time, nearly everyone has some exposure to the other three. In line with the simple terminology used by TA the four positions are known as:

I'm not OK/You're OK,
I'm OK/You're not OK,
I'm not OK/You're not OK, and finally
I'm OK/You're OK.

Clearly the healthy state is the last one and it is this that we can all help ourselves to develop into with knowledge, practice, and mutual support.

In a practical sense simply understanding these concepts can be of great help in making improvements, and there is no reason to suppose that they are beyond anyone's grasp, given the provision of careful, thoughtful training and an emphasis on thinking about the practical usability of the ideas in developing more productive relationships with our customers. Organizations that have trained their staff in these ideas report dramatic changes in attitude for behaviour as well as business results. Some of the airline companies are testimony to this, with Jan Carlzon's brilliant work with Scandinavian Airline Systems leading the way.

Given that we now have a simple language that can be used in helping ourselves and each other, we can next discuss with employees how important it is for us to avoid being defensive in our dealings with customers. A useful tip here is to listen for the two words 'yes but' which so often signal a defensive reaction, either in us or the other person. In either situation it is dangerous and a clear sign of being at least potentially in a win/lose situation.

This aspect of the training in customer orientation, then, focuses on helping us to recognize that there are two ends to every stick and on giving us the awareness of the skills needed to recognize and appreciate what is going on at the other end. It says that if we feel good in ourselves and positive about ourselves, then this will generally translate itself into effective dealings with our customers. Training programmes such as these have been termed 'smiling courses', which is one relevant aspect of the subject. Even smiling down the phone can change the nature of a dialogue very substantially! There are, however, different types of smile, and the other subjects and skills covered here help to ensure that the smile is not a competitive smirk or a hollow charade, but a symbol of genuine pleasure at trying and being able to meet the requirements of our customers.

The second dimension of this training session should be to focus on the skills required for the particular type of dealings that staff have with their customers. It will not be sensible to spend a lot of time teaching someone telephone skills if they literally never use the phone at work, and similarly with written communications. This part of the training therefore needs to be designed in a modular way so that different groups who receive the training can, if necessary, receive different inputs to reflect their particular needs. Again this is not the place to go into the intricate detail of telephone skills training, or the requirement in terms of writing customer letters. It is enough to note that when the analysis of this requirement is complete there are consultancies which specialize in these aspects of training, and there are also specialist books which have been written on the subject which give ideas of appropriate ways to handle the need.

The third dimension of this training which we must mention, of course, is that it is vital to get across the message that even if we develop high levels of skills in all these areas we will still not have done enough until we gear all of our dealings with our customers to agreeing clearly and precisely what their requirements are, and what mechanisms we can use to measure our performance in meeting them. If we ally this to the first and second aspects we have covered then we will be in the process of achieving Excellence in our everyday dealings with the people around us.

Training programmes on this subject should be designed to encourage participants to develop their own monitoring and tracking mechanisms to assist them, and time can usefully be included for this within the programme itself. Furthermore, it is invariably useful to try to encourage people to develop mechanisms for helping each other as they work on improving their skills in this area, and since a part of such mechanisms is likely to be the giving of feedback, it will be important to include training in making this descriptive rather than judgemental. Most people tend to be very evaluative, and this often has the reverse of the intended effect, as it usually throws the recipient onto the defensive and into a blind rejection of the comment or advice. It will be much better for the most part to encourage people to describe their own thoughts and feelings about an issue or someone's behaviour, rather than judging it. The clue here is to remember the input about perceptions and to encourage people to realize that their reaction is only one perception of the many possible ones. We are not in a position therefore to judge right or wrong, just to express our view, with the goal of giving the other person the chance himself of seeing his own behaviour in a different light. Developing our skills in the whole area of feedback can be of enormous value in improving skills in this most vital of areas, and time spent on it in a practical way will be of tremendous long-term value.

This chapter has dealt with an aspect of the Journey to Excellence which many will interpret as being 'soft centred'. In a crude way it will be dismissed by some as 'teaching our people to be nice' and therefore as having no real place in a hard nosed business environment. Do not fall into this trap! It may be 'soft' training, but it is there to achieve very 'hard' results. It is often said that 'nice guys don't win', a statement that equates 'niceness' with 'softness', and is thus nonsensical in any general way. There are large numbers of 'greats' in every field from sport to business, and from rock music to religion, who have international reputations not only for their grit, determination, and general 'hardness' in their chosen field but also for their 'niceness' as human beings. It is also interesting to note that the value systems or organizational philosophies of most Excellent organizations place very heavy emphasis on having respect for people. It is these organizations that win, and continue to win in the long run, not because it is good to be nice but, more pragmatically, because any organization ultimately depends on generating a large measure of self-motivation amongst its staff, and this is more likely to be achieved, and maintained, by organizations that treat people with dignity and respect, whatever their level in the hierarchy. The training requirement which has been discussed in this chapter is fundamental to the achievement of Excellence, because Excellence depends on Quality, Quality is meeting customer requirements, and therefore all employees need to develop high levels of skill in dealing with customers, whether internal or external.

Chapter 14

IN–DEPARTMENT EVALUATION OF ACTIVITIES AND THE COST OF QUALITY

On our Journey to Excellence we will require milestones to enable us to see what progress we are making. We will also need a mechanism to help us get an overview of what happens in the organization at the moment, and what range of opportunities exist for improvement in our quest for Excellence through Quality. The technique which fulfils both these needs is called an in-department evaluation of activity (IDEA).

In an earlier chapter the notion of having a measuring stick to enable us to judge progress was mooted. This measuring stick is the Cost of Quality and it will be appropriate briefly to review this here. The Cost of Quality is, as it sounds, the total amount of money that it costs to ensure that we meet the stated requirements of our customers, and therefore provide Quality goods and services. There are three different costs which make up the Cost of Quality, two of which are costs associated with trying to get it right first time. Firstly, there is the cost of prevention, in other words the things we do to try to prevent defects occurring, and secondly there is the cost of appraisal or detection of defects, which are the costs incurred whilst the organization is going about its planned business activities. Examples of prevention would be any 'one-off' improvements designed to prevent defects in the future, training and planning activities and so on. Examples of costs of appraisal would be the normal sampling and testing which are carried out by Quality Control departments, or any review or control system in any part of the organization.

The third cost associated with Quality is the cost incurred as a result of getting it wrong the first time. This is the cost of failure, and includes anything which happens in the organization which has to be done again, all mistakes and errors, not only on the production side of the organization but in the offices as well. A letter that has to be retyped is just as much a cost of failure as a defective component. Furthermore, the cost of failure will include all guarantee claims and rework as well as any department or activity which is set up to deal with customer complaints, and can include lost customers and the business that goes with them.

In most organizations the Cost of Quality at the beginning of the Journey to Excellence will be somewhere between 20 and 50 per cent of the sales revenue of the company, and the cost of failure will be a large part of this. If we want to achieve Excellence through Quality we need to work on reducing this very significantly, and for us to be able to tackle this in an organized and systematic way we need to be able to measure progress as we go. This is done by keeping track of the cost of Quality on a regular basis.

The second requirement we have at this stage of the process is to establish what is actually happening in the organization at this time, and the extent to which the activities are meeting the stated requirements of our internal and external customers. This will not only give us a measure of what we need to do to provide a Quality service to our internal and external customers but will also generate many specific possibilities for staff to work on either as individuals or groups.

The IDEA mechanism is a powerful technique which fully meets the requirements for this stage of the process. Basically it involves taking an in-depth look at what is happening in a department, and of doing so in an organized and systematic way, so that the findings can be used by management and staff in the department to reduce work on the number of defects in their system. The IDEA process asks a number of questions and explores various issues in depth. To ensure that the data collected are readily usable, it should be recorded in a format which has been carefully designed to facilitate this. It is essential that IDEA analysts are trained in the technique and therefore are able to assist the different departments in using it. Because it is likely that more than one person will be involved in doing this, the format designed should be as standardized as possible to ensure the compatibility of the information being collected.

Ultimately the analysis will include every single activity which is performed in the organization, and so at the outset it will be necessary to plan how this will be handled. The departments, sections, or functions need to be viewed in a way which logically facilitates the process. For example, it is unrealistic to expect that the director of a function in a major corporation will know the intricate details of all the work performed within the function. The same might be said of the senior manager and even the middle manager in the hierarchy. Equally these people perform work functions which must be analysed along with the rest. As a rule of thumb, therefore, the unit of analysis should be the section, that is the work group managed by a first-level supervisor. The offices of the different levels of management and their staff assistants, if they have them, should be viewed as separate units but treated in exactly the same way when it comes to applying the technique.

The first area which is explored by IDEA concerns the work done in the section. This needs to be explored in detail and recorded. A good way of doing this is to begin with a general description of the purpose of the section, what it is there to do, and then to break this down into the tasks and activities which are undertaken. These should be recorded as single sentences and listed separately. It is all too easy to assume that this listing will be instantly accessible in the mind of the supervisor or first-level manager, who is the person being 'interviewed' by the analyst at this stage. Usually it is not, and requires a considerable amount of thinking about, to order the activities in a meaningful way and to remember everything. There are likely to be alterations and changes made to the 'top of the head' assessment of the supervisor and so it is important, firstly, that the analyst is patient, and also that he is prepared to write up a final copy of the documentation after the discussion has ended, and after it has been discussed and possibly amended, as a result of the section meetings which form a later stage in the process.

The stages that follow take each item which has been recorded in turn and subject them to further analysis. The second question to be explored asks about the 'suppliers' and the 'customers' as far as the item is concerned. Another way of putting this is to view it as the interfaces with other work, but since we are engaged in a widescale educational process to get people thinking in terms of internal suppliers and customers it would be unfortunate to lose this opportunity of reinforcing the message. The questions then relate to 'who are the suppliers who provide the inputs for this piece of work' and secondly 'who are the customers that the outputs of the work will be passed to when we have finished them'. The answers should be recorded. By tracking the flow of answers to these questions we can check whether people are accurately identifying their suppliers and customers and also we can get a very useful overview of the business processes that are the lifeblood of the organization. We should not be too surprised either if there are some examples of sections which do not know, or wrongly assess, the answers to these questions, since this may be the first time that people have really thought of what they do in this way.

The third area of the analysis looks at the extent to which the requirements of the customers have been specified. Remembering that quality is 'meeting stated customer requirements now and in the future', it is essential that these requirements are both discussed and recorded in an organized way. In many cases there will not have been meetings between supplier and customer to specify the customer's requirements, and where this is the case it will not be possible to complete the IDEA procedure at this first meeting. Asking the question, however, will trigger a discussion and a second meeting should be scheduled immediately, to complete the analysis. The idea at this stage is to look both backwards and forwards. We need, for each activity we undertake, to meet our suppliers and specify our requirements as customers. Secondly, we need, again for each activity we undertake, to meet with our customers to specify their requirements so that we can work in an organized way to meet them.

The fourth question builds on from the third, and utilizes one of the key principles of this new Quality concept, which is basically that if it is not measured, both for us as customers and suppliers, then it is not Quality. When we have specified and quantified the requirements we next require mechanisms for measuring and tracking the extent to which the requirements are met—in other words the Quality of the input we receive from our suppliers and the output we pass on to our customers. The questions here relate to which are the important measurements, and whether they have been established and are in place. If they have, we need to note down what they are and the format used for displaying them—graphs, histograms, control charts, etc. Furthermore, it is important to note down the frequency of the measurement. If no mechanisms are in place the discussion should attempt to identify what measures should be introduced, what form they should take, and with what frequency they should be produced. These should be introduced by the line manager, and the recording system used for IDEA should highlight when the tracking system is in place and being used routinely. In the early stages of the IDEA process, it may be necessary for the analyst to advise management or the supervisor as to the most appropriate formats for the tracking systems. Progressively, however, as managers and employees are trained in problem-solving skills and basic measurement techniques, they will be able to fulfil this requirement themselves.

The fifth area of analysis relates to the amount of people's time which is spent on work related to the cost of Quality—in other words, time spent on prevention, appraisal, and failure. To assist in this part of the analysis, whoever is carrying out the IDEA needs to have access to the standard costs for people's time at different levels of the organization so that times can easily be converted to money. As a lead in to this part of the discussion with the supervisor it should first be established how much time is spent on the activity in total. This can be expressed in hours per week, month, or year, as appropriate to the task. Any unusual feature which affects the time spent should be noted, for example some tasks are only performed once a year or are seasonal.

Having established this, the next step is to establish whether or not the activity is a Cost of Quality or a 'cost of doing business'. What is meant here is that in any organization the activities performed can be viewed in one of four categories. The first three are the three Costs of Quality which have already been discussed, the cost of preventing defects and errors, the cost of appraising or inspecting work, and the cost of producing failures or errors. The fourth type of cost is that associated with actually producing defect-free goods and services and of running the business. So the time taken to perform any task can be analysed under these four headings. Many tasks will involve more than one heading, some will be entirely a Cost of Quality, and others will be entirely a 'cost of doing business'. If the task is a Cost of Quality, either entirely or in part, the next step is carefully to establish, with the manager or supervisor which category or categories it should go in and how much time is spent in each category. At the beginning, this is likely to prove quite difficult until people get into the swing of thinking in this way, but it becomes much easier with practice. In the early stages it will be useful to have the definitions of the different costs written down for reference, together with some examples of each, which may help in the making of the judgement. The lists that follow are designed to assist in this respect.

Examples of costs of prevention include:

Quality training programmes
Planning systems and planning meetings
Time spent thinking about improvement possibilities to reduce and avoid defects
    next time
Quality team meetings
One-off purchases of tools, equipment, or systems which are designed to facilitate
    getting the job right first time
One-off, non-standard evaluation of performance to highlight problems/opportunities

.n general terms anything which is designed to facilitate the job being done right the first time comes within this category.

Costs of appraisal include:

Standard sampling of products
Standard testing and inspection procedures
Routine departmental control documentation
Routine audits
Proof reading memos and other documents

In general terms any situation where someone does a piece of work and someone else checks it will be included here.

Costs of failure include:

All rework in all departments, including clerical and sales functions, not just production
All errors in all departments
Cost of claims under guarantee and the administration of such claims
Customer complaint departments
Any unplanned 'emergency' activity
Lost business through dissatisfied customers
Time spent chasing people, repeat calls, etc.

In general terms reacting to or replacing work which was not done right first time will be included here.

It is not necessary that this Cost of Quality analysis is 100 per cent accurate. It is not a strict financial measure and the most important idea is that it acts as a consistent measure of progress. Consistency is more important, therefore, than either the precise degree of accuracy we achieve or for that matter that every single aspect of the Cost of Quality has been included. If we can achieve an 80 per cent accuracy and coverage, but can ensure a 95 per cent level of consistency in the analysis, we will be fulfilling our requirements for the mechanism. It really is important therefore that the documentation which is used in this process is suitable since it will need to be used again and again as future Cost of Quality 'audits' take place. On this subject the measurement of the Cost of Quality needs to take place regularly to give us feedback about progress; specifically this should be every four to six months initially. Depending on the organization, this level of frequency can be adapted after the first two or three years, but should never be allowed to be less frequent than twice a year and ideally it should be a monthly figure.

Thus far the steps of the IDEA process have helped us to look at what happens in the section or department, who the suppliers and customers are for each of the activities which are undertaken, whether or not the requirements of the customers have been specified, whether or not there are ongoing mechanisms in place for keeping track of the performance of the supplier in meeting the requirements of the customer, and finally the extent to which the activity involves a Cost of Quality, either wholly or in part. This has all been achieved in discussion with the manager or supervisor of the section.

The next step is for the manager to convene a meeting of all staff in the section with the purpose firstly of checking that the job holders are in broad agreement with the analysis so far, and secondly of generating a list of possibilities for improvement. It will normally be appropriate for the analyst to attend this discussion since the paperwork may need amending as a result of the discussion. This stage will normally take place after staff have been trained in the basic concepts which form this new approach, so there will be some understanding of the ideas which underlie the analysis. It will, however, be useful at the outset to summarize the new concept to serve as a reminder for staff, and either the supervisor or the analyst can undertake this task. It should be established, in working on the first objective of the meeting, that the aim is not to get embroiled in an argument about semantics. Most activities can be described in different ways depending on the style and the perception of the individual. It is more important that the full range of work accomplished in the section is included, however it is described, remembering that the Cost of Quality analysis which is one of the outputs of the analysis will be used quite frequently to give us a measure of progress, and therefore needs to be capable of providing a consistent base for the measurement.

Finally, and normally within the same meeting, the whole group should be involved in generating a list of possible improvements which could be made in the section to rid it of defects and therefore be more successful in meeting the requirements of the customers. The best mechanism for this stage is to use the technique of brainstorming. This will necessitate either training people in the technique or at least of reminding them of the rules. The question which should form the focus for the session should be 'What are all the ways we can improve the performance of our section?' Brainstorming sessions should be short and 'explosive', lasting no longer than about 20 or 25 minutes. The idea at this stage is simply to generate a long list of possibilities, not to evaluate the list or to decide on priorities. As we have already stated, the IDEA process helps us to audit the current actitivities of the organization within the framework which is necessary for us to achieve Excellence through Quality. It also gives us a measure against which to view our success. We are now ready to start some Quality activities which will help us in the first action phase of our Journey to Excellence.

The IDEA process then will certainly involve two meetings, one with the manager and one with the manager and his staff. It may well involve one or two additional discussions if there are aspects highlighted by the first interview which are not currently being tackled. IDEA is not designed to be a trap or a test, and it is very important that it is not perceived as such by the managers and supervisors in the organization. The first few meetings that are held are likely to reveal that considerable work needs to be done to put ourselves on the road to achieving Excellence through Quality. Many sections will not have specified requirements from their suppliers and with their customers. This must not be taken as a weakness or failing on the part of the manager or the staff, and equally with the question relating to the measurement of activities. This new concept requires new thinking and new ways of doing things throughout the organization and it would be difficult to believe that all of these aspects were already being fully covered.

A further aspect of this important topic is that there may be an initial tendency for people to underestimate the amount of failure that there is currently and to overstate the prevention activities already in place. This will not help either the section or the organization. Firstly, the standard measurements of conformance to customer requirements which are introduced in the section will reveal the level of defects, and it will be clear that something is amiss if no time is going into correcting them. Secondly, since the whole process we are involved in is a journey, it is not expected that we should be halfway to our destination at the outset. Remember what Lao Tse, the Chinese philosopher said, 'The journey of a thousand miles starts with one step'. These are among our first steps on this endless journey. They are likely to be a little faltering, but since Excellence itself is a journey rather than a destination we begin to achieve Excellence as we start the trek. It will be better to be open and honest from the outset, and to focus attention on making progress along the road, and everyone should be reminded of this during these discussions.

Once the IDEA discussions have taken place the analysts will need to work with the data which has been generated, since they contain much which will be of value in promoting Quality activities.

The key analyses which need to be made are, firstly, to piece together the pattern of suppliers and customers, to establish whether there are any misconceptions, and also to find out where there is a need for meetings to take place to specify requirements. Where there are gaps, it is the responsibility of line management to fill them, but the Quality staff can often play a useful facilitating role.

The next analysis concerns measurement. There will usually be a need for Quality staff to assist in the process of developing control mechanisms. These are needed to track the progress being made in departments towards meeting customer requirements through achieving defect-free work consistently. Again it is a line management responsibility to set up and maintain an appropriate monitoring system, but Quality staff can provide useful technical information about, and training in, the different mechanisms available.

The third analysis relates to the ideas that have been generated for improvement. Quality staff will need to look at the lists of ideas with a view to isolating any common themes that run through them. This will enable them to report back to the main steering committee specifically regarding Quality task forces which are needed to tackle such issues.

Fourthly, the Quality manager will need to calculate the Cost of Quality. A lot of the input for this figure comes directly from the IDEA and is a matter of adding up the individual departmental assessments of costs of prevention, appraisal, and failure. The next step is to gather together information about other dimensions of this cost, the physical costs associated with failure. These include such things as claims under guarantee, unnecessary scrap from the department, including, for example, the wasted paper from the offices and wasted food from the company restaurant, the costs of 'give-aways' to ameliorate dissatisfied customers, and so on, as well as the production scrap costs, which are the only ones normally measured. In doing this it is very important that the assumptions made are noted since we will want to be comparing like with like when the Cost of Quality analysis is repeated, to give us feedback about our performance over a period of time. This is made more important because the analysis is not a strict financial one and there is no built-in check as there is with the true financial statements and double-entry bookkeeping systems. It is, frankly, perfectly normal to miss things which are actually Costs of Quality when the analysis is done for the first few times, and it is important therefore that Quality staff are in control of the assumptions behind the calculation. Otherwise, as people get more used to doing Cost of Quality analyses and include more aspects in it, the overall figure may show a worsening trend even though real improvements are being made. There is no desire here to show anything but an accurate figure. The recognition that the true figure for Cost of Quality is a larger proportion of sales acts as a motivator when it is realized that this gives us more to do, more opportunities for improvement.

Having said this we do not want to demotivate people by showing a worsening trend, if in fact the trend is an improving one, so some retrospective amendments will probably be needed to be able to compare like with like.

The in-department evaluation of activities is an essential springboard into Quality improvement activities. Building on the basic Quality awareness education programme and the customer orientation training, this stage not only reinforces the message of the new concept but also brings it into an even more vivid perspective, and probably most important, it leaves the departments, the managers, and the staff with many tangible and stated opportunities which are within their own grasp, and which direct their first steps on their own Journey to Excellence. The next stage is to give people the tools to do the job.

Part 4

GETTING THINGS DONE—
THE BUILDERS

Chapter 15

GETTING THINGS DONE AS INDIVIDUALS AND GROUPS

There are four basic types of group activity which are needed to achieve Excellence through Quality. They are all different and are designed to fulfil different roles in the process. At the outset it is very important to understand that they are all precise mechanisms and that if the features of any of the groups are changed, it changes the whole concept on which that group has been based. This chapter discusses the format of these four types of activity, but before going on to this it is appropriate to emphasize this last point since it has been the cause of failure of many such activities. An example comes from one large organization which was interested in introducing a Quality Circle programme into one of its plants. Such was the enthusiasm of management for the concept that they became impatient and decided that the recommended slow and steady introduction of Quality Circles on a voluntary basis was not for them. They introduced a programme which broke some of the core principles of the approach, notably its voluntary nature for all employees, and furthermore they tried to run before they could walk by introducing a lot of groups at once. What happened was both predictable and tragic. The programme, of course, failed within six or nine months, but in a sense it was even worse than that for the unions involved to this day refuse even to discuss Quality Circles with management. The tragedy here is that not only was a great opportunity missed but it produced a bizarre happening in that the union, in this case, refused to discuss a concept about which it has no experience.

Certainly the programme which was introduced was called Quality Circles, but it was not Quality Circles; it was light years away from it. Increasingly there are companies which have introduced the Quality Circle concept that are finding it diffi-cult to sustain in the longer term. At the root of such difficulties is very often the fact that what they introduced was not Quality Circles and that the short-lived nature of the phenomenon which was tried was actually entirely predictable had a bit of foresight been applied at the outset. Quality Circles are one of the key mechanisms in achieving Excellence and are dealt with in more detail later in this chapter, and so the example is very relevant. At this point, though, the example is designed to illustrate how important it is to stay within the design of the different groups which play such a central role in the process.

The first two types of group are called Quality Task Forces and Quality Department Groups. They are similar in every respect except that a Quality Task Force is a cross-functional group usually set up by a senior manager or the steering committee, whereas the Quality Department Group is a group established by the manager in a department or section to solve an 'in-house' problem, and generally contains mem-bers of the department, though it is possible to include others with relevant knowledge and skills where appropriate. One of the core Quality concepts is that the approach operates through management, and must do, because 80 per cent of the opportunities for improvement are controlled by management and therefore require management action of some sort. Therefore it is an essential ingredient that management are able to establish groups to work on Quality issues, whether they be problems or opportunities.

The first feature of a Quality Task Force or Quality Department Group, therefore, is that it is a group formed to look at a specific issue which a manager believes is important and warrants investigation in this way. The setting up of such a group will often be the work of such a manager, though it is likely that the Quality Steering Groups will also see issues which can be tackled via such mechanisms, and they should certainly be authorized to establish such activities. These are then designed as 'one-off' groups which are set up to look at a specific subject and to report back.

The second feature of this type of group concerns ownership. Clearly in this case the real ownership rests with the person or body that inititated the activity in the first place. This is an important feature to bear in mind with any group activity, since it is likely to affect the deep-down commitment that people have towards the subject in hand. People tend to be more committed to activities that they feel they own themselves. These groups are not expected to generate high levels of ownership and commitment, if they do it is a bonus. The main purpose here is to have an important issue investigated in a thorough manner by a group of suitably qualified employees.

The selection of members of the group is the third feature to note, and the key here is to understand that people are selected to be part of the activity. There is no question here of anything being voluntary. Of course the wise manager or steering group will ensure that the people chosen for membership are encouraged and helped to be interested in the project, but at the end of the day the people to do the job will be chosen according to their potential contribution as far as this particular question is concerned.

Fourthly, the composition of the group, in most cases, is likely to include people from different parts of the organization if it is a Quality Task Force, whereas with a Quality Department Group it will normally be contained within one manager's area of authority. The cross-functional nature of most Quality Task Force activities reflects the role of senior management and the steering groups in the process of achieving Excellence, which is to take a 'helicopter view' and to be able to identify necessary activities which are not directly the job of any one department or section. Equally the manager of any department also needs this helicopter ability, and uses it in forming Quality Department Groups in his area as required.

Fifthly, the precise formulation of these groups will vary according to the particular issue being investigated, but in terms of size should never exceed the traditionally accepted limits of a small group, which is to say ten people. If more than ten people are involved in a problem-solving activity, the dynamics of the group begin to get very complex, and invariably reduce the effectiveness of the work accomplished. The group should meet as often as is dictated by the size, importance, and urgency of the question under review and the duration of the group's existence will be affected by similar considerations. One thing that is important, however, is that the owners of this activity, management or a steering group, must establish the boundaries of the task at the outset, and this must include a date by which the report is due. This means that everyone is clear as to the requirements, and can gear their work to meeting those requirements in an organized and systematic way.

Quality Task Forces and Quality Department Groups will be used in a wide range of situations. It is likely that there will always be such groups on the go as new issues, problems, and opportunities need to be addressed. As a device they are similar to project groups which are used by many organizations already, but they have a distinct advantage over the majority of such activities in that members of the group will be trained in, and will use, a Quality problem-solving structure and a range of Quality analytical tools and techniques. An absolutely vital requirement for all these group activities is that members are trained in how to identify, analyse, and solve problems, how to work together effectively in groups, how to present their findings, and how to control and monitor results. A brief outline of what needs to be included in such training is given in Chapter 16 of this book, entitled 'The problem-solving structure'.

The third type of activity which is essential in the Journey to Excellence is Quality Circles. The nature of Quality Circles is such that it is more of a concept in its own right than merely being another different type of group. As such it is important to understand the approach in some detail since it is the mechanism for accomplishing much of what has been missed in previous models for creating change in organizations, since it focuses on giving staff the opportunity to become genuinely involved in the process.

This book is not the place for a full-scale treatise on the Quality Circles concept since there are books which have been specifically written for this. It is certainly appropriate, however, to cover the subject in some detail since it is such a vital part of the Journey to Excellence.

The Quality Circle concept is a universal one with literally millions of people involved covering all continents of the world. Though Quality Circles first developed in Japan during the late 1950s and early 1960s, the approach is actually based on Western theories of management, notably Douglas McGregor's Theory Y.

At the outset it is important to understand how Quality Circles should be viewed and what place the concept should have in an organization, for if it is treated merely as another management technique it is unlikely to stand the test of time. If introduced properly the Quality Circles concept represents part of a coherent managerial philosophy which aims at 'gathering the wisdom of the people', which is how the Japanese describe these groups. It is not a 'stand alone' concept, but forms one aspect of the way we want to do things as we travel on the Journey to Excellence. In a sentence, Quality Circles is an approach which allows employees to become more involved, by solving their own job-related problems in an organized way. It sounds simple, but in fact this is deceptive, and if we analyse the definition, we can isolate a number of reasons for this. Firstly, Quality Circles is an approach which allows people to get more involved, but puts no pressure on them to do so; in other words the approach is entirely voluntary at all levels of the organization. This principle of voluntariness is crucial to the success of Quality Circles, so much so that we can state categorically that if it is not voluntary then it is not Quality Circles. It is, however, not an easy thing to introduce and to manage, since it is such an unusual notion. In the working life of the average employee one rather suspects that nothing is really voluntary, and yet this is, but it takes more than a mere statement to make the principle a reality. This is not simply a whim. The voluntary principle is crucial because the activity is designed to give ownership to a level of employee that previously has 'owned' very little in an organizational sense. The ownership of Quality Circles groups is very genuinely with the members of the group, unlike Quality Task Forces which we established are owned by the manager or steering group that sets them up.

Quality Circle groups choose the problems they wish to deal with, they choose when to meet and how to work, and ultimately whether they want to continue. Giving ownership in this way is the only real way of demonstrating and building on the existing level of trust in the organization, and it is the most effective way of developing the high levels of commitment amongst people which are essential to the attainment of Excellence.

The second distinctive feature of the Quality Circle approach is that the people who join in are encouraged to solve their own job-related problems. When asked to state what problems affect them at work, most people tend to point to difficulties caused by other sections, departments, or people, rather than to things that lie within their own sphere of influence. This inevitably causes frustration and tends to be a circular process since for every finger pointed there tends to be at least one pointing back. Quality Circles overcome this major difficulty of participative problem solving by introducing the combined ideas of 'no finger pointing' and 'put your own house in order'. By focusing on issues that they can influence Quality Circles are in a much stronger position to get things done than if they spend their time trying to tell others what to do.

The third feature of the Quality Circles definition which is worthy of comment is that they solve their problems in an organized way; in other words they are given training in the skills of systematic problem solving and of working together effectively in a group. Quality Circles is probably the only approach which gives such training to non-supervisory staff. Training is a key part of the concept since it gives members the tools to do the job. It should be remembered that for most staff this will be the first time that they will have been involved in such an activity, and it would be very dangerous to assume that the requisite skills were already in place and ready to be used. Indeed, it is difficult to see how a Quality Circles programme could really succeed without training being an integral part of it.

So it can be seen that the approach is not nearly as simple as it seems. It needs to form a part of the philosophy of management of the organization, and it must be voluntary, with the focus on 'putting our own house in order'. Furthermore, training must be given to enable groups to engage in the problem-solving activity in an organized and professional way. So much for the overall concept. In rather more detail, a Quality Circle consists of a group of four to ten volunteers who work for the same first line supervisor and who meet together regularly to identify, analyse, and solve their work problems. A number of points are worth highlighting.

Firstly, the Quality Circles concept is a natural work group approach as distinct from a task force or project group process. It is a key part of the design of Circles that members all work for the same supervisor and that the work they do is similar or that the jobs have logical connections with each other. The second point worth highlighting is that the group does not need to consist of the entire workforce from that section. If twenty people work in an area and nine volunteer, then the nine form the Quality Circle. Of course, the remaining eleven must be kept informed at all times about the topics being tackled, and indeed they should be encouraged to put forward their ideas even if they do not want to join the group.

Thirdly, the groups meet regularly once a week, for an hour, and as far as possible in paid time. Once a week is a good practical balance between the desire to get on with things, on the one hand, and the need to ensure that the work flow in the section is not adversely affected, on the other. The meetings should be limited in length, as an antidote to Parkinson's law, experience showing that an hour is the right length of time in most circumstances. Finally, on this subject, the meetings should be held in paid time. This is because they are about work, not leisure, and as such should be paid in the normal way, no more, no less.

Fourthly, the groups at their meetings do not stop at the identification of problems for passing on to management to solve. They utilize the training they receive to analyse and solve them, and then to present their findings to management. Having been successful in having their ideas accepted the group will usually be responsible for implementation, and will always monitor the results of the solution to check that it has worked. The group then decides on the next issue to tackle, because Quality Circles is an ongoing activity, in contrast to the QTFs which are specifically set up to deal with one issue and then disband.

Turning to the objectives of a Quality Circles programme, there are three main goals: those of staff involvement, people development, and the achievement of tangible benefits. For encouraging direct involvement across a broad front, quite simply the Quality Circles concept stands alone as the best mechanism available to organizations today. The second objective is the development of people in the organization. Quality Circles undoubtedly promote the development of staff, through the acquisition of new skills and the opportunity to work together on real world problems, and they also help supervisors to build their problem-solving skills and their abilities in working in and leading small groups. Furthermore, for many managers, Quality Circles offer the practical framework for introducing and developing genuinely participative management styles. While based on sound theoretical premises, the approach is intensely practical, and this is its great strength.

The third goal of Quality Circles is to generate benefits for the organization and the people in it. The evidence suggests that Quality Circles programmes tend to be cost effective and sometimes very much so. Paybacks of up to fifteen times the investment have occasionally been reported. A vital concern about this, however, is that it is very dangerous to make this objective the primary one, since doing so will involve putting pressure on, and maybe breaking, some of the rules, notably that the groups decide which problem to tackle; there must therefore be no pressure on them to select only ones which have a direct tangible benefit. If this happens, the ownership of the group has been 'stolen' and the concept becomes nothing more than another management controlled and regulated technique.

Quality Circles work on a very wide range of issues over which they have some influence. They are a key ingredient within any section or department in the quest for meeting customer requirements now and in the future, since the members are closest to the activities which will help this to come about. This is why the groups need to be ongoing, for there is always work to be done.

The three types of group covered so far, Quality Task Forces, Quality Department Groups, and Quality Circles, are central to the achievement of Excellence, but there is yet a need for one more formulation to enable us to meet every eventuality. This fourth type of group is called a Quality Improvement Team and again is constructed in a precise way to fulfil a precise need. In organizations, people are not only concerned about their own activities and problems; often they have interests in a wide range of problems, possibilities, and opportunities which affect them, but require other people to be involved with them as well if any progress is to be made. Some of these issues may not be high enough on the list of priorities for top management to establish a Quality Task Force, and indeed in many cases this would not be an appropriate method of dealing with the issue. In a nutshell, there is a need for a mechanism which allows employees, including management, to work on issues of interest and concern to them, in groups which they own. Quality Circles fulfil this requirement within the work group, whilst Quality Improvement Teams deal with it where the need goes across departmental or functional boundaries. Again we are talking here of a precise mechanism, and so it is important to spell out dimensions of this kind of group.

The first aspect of Quality Improvement Teams that is important to state is that, like Quality Circles, membership is voluntary. We have already stated in the section on Quality Circles that this is more than a whim. Making something voluntary means that there is a far greater likelihood of people who join in being committed to it. A practical expression of the voluntary nature is in the vesting of ownership with the group. Within the broad guidelines set down, group members have a free reign in exploring the subject of their concern.

The second notable feature is that Quality Improvement Teams are based on specific issues. These can be problems or opportunities, it does not matter; the important point to note is that the group forms to look at one issue. Once the issue has been dealt with the group disbands. With a Quality Task Force, the time scale involved in exploring the issue selected by management is unlikely to be more than a few months in most circumstances, and there will be Quality Improvement Teams for whom this is also the case. There are likely to be other subjects, however, which necessitate the group continuing its activity for a much longer period of time, and indeed there may be some which need to be ongoing. To a large extent the issue itself will determine this since, with a voluntary group, membership will quickly fall away once the job has been done and there is therefore no remaining interest in the work.

It should be said, though, that the members of Quality Improvement Teams, because it is their group, can continue to meet for as long as they think fit, and as long as they perceive there is value in pursuing the topic further. So, unlike Quality Circles, the group does not select another problem to work on once the initial problem has been solved. Members of the group may, of course, opt to be members of another Quality Improvement Team that forms to work on a different issue, but the original group disbands once its job has been done.

The third aspect of Quality Improvement Teams concerns their composition. As far as members are concerned the only limit should be that of a small group—in other words, up to ten people. The group should be allowed to meet for a maximum of one hour per week, and the understanding should be that members should spend less time if they believe it to be appropriate. An important aspect of these groups is that everyone in the organization ultimately should be given the chance to belong to one, since they represent a very useful way of encouraging the involvement of all staff and of developing commitment to solving a wide range of organizational problems. The membership of these groups does not usually come just from one work area; they are, more often than not, cross-functional. Furthermore, representation from different levels in the organization, including management, should be encouraged wherever possible and appropriate. This not only helps to ensure a rounded analysis and proposal for improvement, but also helps to reinforce communication up and down the organization as well as across the functional boundaries.

These groups, like Quality Circles, are not likely to be currently in use in most organizations, certainly in this form and dealing with these kind of Quality-related issues. An absolute key to the success of Quality Improvement Teams is that they are task-orientated groups that use a systematic problem-solving structure to ensure a professional treatment of their subjects. Many organizations have intuitively recognized the need for such groups, especially from the point of view of communication, and have set up what could be called 'tea and biscuits' or 'coffee and danish' groups! These are usually unstructured and informal meetings, which are scheduled to take place regularly and to promote a free flow of information between departments and people. They usually start off very well with a high level of interest and involvement. Progressively, however, attendance tails off when it becomes clear that nothing is really getting done as a result of the meetings, and gradually they tend to fade away, unless a particularly strong person forces attendance, thus making it more of a briefing meeting than a voluntary group. This is not to say that such activities are a waste of time, for often benefits derive from the early meetings as people are able to get a perspective that had eluded them in the past. The reality is, however, that such mechanisms, though set up to be permanent institutions, tend to fade away very quickly. This often has an effect on the perception which people have of them. If something is set up to be a permanent feature of the organization and it transpires not to be, many will see it as a failure, even if progress is made. One of the key aspects of learning that has emerged in these processes over the past few years has been how important it is to establish what expectations we can realistically have of these different group activities, and to be very clear about them from the outset. In the case in point it would be much better to set up such a system for a defined period of time, say four or six weeks, since any gains made in that time will be perceived positively and not be tainted in any way by the planned demise of the group itself. So the key point here is that Quality Improvement Teams are not discussion groups; they need to be very task orientated and they need to use an organized and systematic approach to the analysis and solution of the problems in hand.

Clearly group working will not be the appropriate mechanism for handling all of the problems and opportunities that will need tackling on the journey. Groups are a powerful way of working when they work effectively, and as long as the issues are conducive to being tackled by more than one person. This is not always the case, and since we want to avoid groups of people sitting down to invent the horse and coming up with the camel, we need a mechanism to assist individuals to work on Quality issues in an organised and systematic fashion. Such a system can be called by many names, one being the 'Individual Quest for Quality'. The detail of what such a system should include is given in Chapter 17 of this book, and it is an essential complement to the group working structures which are dealt with in the rest of this chapter.

Chapter 16

THE PROBLEM–SOLVING STRUCTURE

There are many problems, even in the best run of organizations, and there are even more opportunities for making things even better than they are currently as we wend our way on the Journey to Excellence and defect-free performance in everything we do. Given this, it is surprising that most people and organizations tend not to use any form of problem-solving structure or organized methodology for exploiting opportunities. As a result, we tend, broadly speaking to tackle problems by 'bumbling through' using a mixture of intuition and experience. Typically, many people tend to think that they 'know' the answer because they have a 'gut feeling' for the situation, based on however many years they have spent in the section, department, or organization. Unfortunately, of course, not everyone has the same 'gut feeling', and we are by no means assured of the right solution using this method, but it is a time-worn one and is used extensively by the majority of organizations. The fact that this method does achieve a proportion of good results is a tribute to the talent which exists in organizations, but, as Picasso said, 'Talent without technique is just a bad habit!' Because people have different intuitive reactions to a subject, whether it be a problem or an opportunity, and because there always seems to be a pressing need to get something done, rather than to spend time thinking and analysing, there is an allied need for agreed decision-making processes. Of course, the simplest situation, and one which many organizations try to promote, is the 'one-on-one' hierarchical decision. This can usually be subtitled the 'you do agree with me, don't you?' method, from boss to subordinate. This game has subtleties of course; for example when the boss, having given his preferred solution, says, 'come on, be open and honest, I really want to hear your views'. This is translated and heard by the subordinate as, 'you do agree with me don't you?', and the mental reaction is often, 'you must be joking!'

on both counts—one the plea for openness and two, the preferred solution. At least, however, this method is safe, in the sense both that it reinforces the present hierarchy and it also protects, and often rewards, the diffident subordinate. When the ideas fail, it is always easy to point to outside circumstances, intervening factors, other people's attitudes, and so on, to justify that it really was the right thing to do at the time!

An alternative to this decision-making process is to work in groups, but as far as group working is concerned, many organizations shy away from it because it is rather more dangerous than the one-on-one mechanism outlined above. Maybe there is an intuitive worry about losing control or getting the 'wrong' answer (defined as someone else's rather than mine!). Other organizations cannot see the point of asking a number of people to do something which they assume would be done more efficiently by one. Even those that do use group working often fall into similar traps as the boss/subordinate example quoted above. Groups meet and decisions are made on the basis of the loudest, most powerful voice. The call from this person 'for everyone's honest view' is heard as often as 'And risk exposure and ridicule in public? You must be joking, I'll keep my head down thank you!' Thus a consensus of silence develops which goes along with the loudest voice. Again, the game is subtle, for when the initiative collapses, the proposer rationalizes that 'they had their chance', whilst the others inwardly muse that they 'could have told him it wouldn't work'. Anyone who claims that such things do not happen with distressing frequency in his organization is either living in a fool's paradise or has spent a lot of time and effort, over a long period, in organized training of people at all levels to develop a range of specific skills in group working designed to avoid this kind of behaviour, for the behaviour is natural and intuitive in most people.

Of course, when writing in this way, one is exposed to the reaction that these, or whatever other methods used, have been successful to date, so why rock the boat? The answer is that these methods do not use the resources which are being utilized in the most effective way, and they lead to defects in our working together which we can increasingly ill afford. In practice, they will often, rather than helping to meet the requirements of our customers, actively work against them. It is sad but true, so what can be done? There are three major areas of concern which need tackling. One is the state of mind that people bring to problem-solving and opportunity-gathering activities; the second is the lack of an organized and systematic structure for handling the issue; and third is the lack of skill most of us display in working together in small groups. This latter point of course is only relevant in dealing with issues where group working is appropriate. There are very many issues which are far better tackled by individuals and it is essential not to get into the syndrome of setting up groups to decide everything. Equally there are undoubtedly a wide range of issues where the best available solution will come out of a group, if that group works effectively. The first two concerns are relevant in the field of both individual and group working and the third is specific to the latter.

First of all it is essential that the state of mind that people bring to the problem-solving process is one which is conducive to getting things done. This involves more than just raw determination since in some circumstances this alone can be very counterproductive. Many groups founder in their work because they spend much of their time blaming other outside parties, or indeed members of their group, for the ills of the world and the specific problem being dealt with. This is not only fruitless, it is also extremely frustrating to all, and so it really is essential that a rule of 'no finger pointing' is agreed and instituted in all work that is done on Quality and Excellence issues.

The second aspect of our state of mind that is so vital is that people should not make assumptions about what others are thinking, or indeed what people outside their particular work area or quality groups might be thinking. If we want to know what people are thinking, then we should go and ask. Many people seriously inhibit their flexibility, the extent of their potential influence, and the success of their proposals by making unwarranted assumptions about the way others would, or do, think. Examples of this include, 'he would never agree to it' or 'they wouldn't understand' or 'I know how they think' or 'I know what you're thinking'.

The third aspect of our state of mind that it is important constantly to be aware of is that this whole process is designed to make our organization Excellent, and that we inhibit this if we fall into internal win/lose conflicts. To do this only serves to help our outside competitors and so developing a win/win frame of mind within our organization is the order of the day on the whole of the Journey to Excellence. All of these aspects form an essential framework within which individuals and groups can become effective. It is worth pointing out that it is only the effectiveness of the work which staff perform which we are concerned with here; we are not concerned with creating a nice, safe, cosy, but unproductive environment. These ingredients are essential to getting things done and sustaining progress on the Journey to Excellence. They represent aspects of hard-nosed management which are fundamental.

The second aspect of concern in involving people in problem-solving activities is that many individuals and groups do not use organized structures or mechanisms when working on problems or opportunities. This unfortunately often means that the quality of the end proposal or action is very much in the lap of the gods. To be Excellent we need to be certain, and this involves helping people to tackle problems in a more organized way. A clear and key rule of quality is that 'if it is not measured it is not quality'. Any work which is done under this banner must be based on facts not opinions, and must be evaluated and monitored in an organized way. This is not a recipe for 'paralysis by analysis' incidentally, since we are talking here of using simple, unbureaucratic mechanisms to assist us, and we are also talking, ultimately, of training everyone in the organization to be able to deal with simple measurement techniques so that they can look after their own needs and track their own progress in meeting the requirements of their own customers.

The second general consideration regarding the use of a problem-solving structure is that it should encourage a suitable blend of both analytical and creative thinking. All too often issues are looked at merely from the logical and obvious points of view, thus missing many other, more creative and possibly more appropriate solutions. This will not always be the case and we are not saying that the creative solution will always be feasible, just that unless we generate ideas that were hitherto unthought of we will not even consider them.

The recommended basic structure which, ultimately, everyone in the organization will need to be trained in contains nine steps, of which the first is to identify the problem or opportunity to be tackled. This can be done by generating lists of possibilities through techniques such as brainstorming, if it is a Quality Circle or a Quality Improvement Team that will be working on the issue, or it can simply be a management requirement, if it is to be the subject of a Quality Department Group or a Quality Task Force.

The second stage is one which is often neglected, or performed badly, both by individuals and groups, and concerns the definition of the issue being tackled. All too often people work on issues which are in fact defined in the form of solutions rather than problems, or problems that are defined in such broad and generalized terms that everyone has a different perception of their meaning. Equally groups or individuals working on opportunities to make things even better often define their goal in terms that do not assist them, terms that are too general and insufficiently quantified. A technique such as that known as Occam's razor can help here.

The third step, having defined the issue clearly, is to have an initial look at it and to try uncovering all of the possible causes of the problem or influences on the opportunity. In the normal run of events, this is done, by both individuals and groups, in a purely analytical way which results in a rather flat, colourless analysis lacking in depth and originality. Of course successful solutions are very often forthcoming from such analyses, but there are also many occasions where better possibilities have been missed. Since many problems and opportunities in organizations concern issues which have been apparent for a long time, and have often been the subject of scrutiny before, it is increasingly necessary that we are able to view them from additional, and maybe less obvious, perspectives. Thus techniques which encourage creative thinking form a core of the proposed problem-solving structure. At this stage we are trying to look at all of the possible causes or influences that could affect the issue, and simple techniques such as the 'bubble diagram' or the 'cause and effect' diagram are designed to assist this. Building on the technique of brainstorming, both the bubble diagram and the cause and effect technique give a loose structure for people to use in recording possibilities and building on previous ideas.

Having looked at the subject from all possible perspectives the fourth step is to use existing knowledge and experience relating to the issue to determine what are felt to be the significant, or so-called 'Pareto', items which affect the issue at hand.

Of course at this stage we are still in the realms of opinion, and so the objective here is to highlight these issues and then to collect data about them in an organized way. Having ensured that the data collected really do give a true and complete picture of the issue being tackled, the fifth step is to interpret what the data are telling us. Here a whole array of mechanisms can be of use, but often the simple expedients of plotting the data in visual forms are sufficient. Histograms, Pareto charts, and other forms of graph are most commonly used here, and simple tests for statistical significance are also helpful at this stage.

Next we need to use a technique such as the six-word diagram or a cause and effect diagram to look for real causes based on our interpretation of the data. This forms step six of the process.

Having established the main causes of the problem or factors affecting the issue based on fact, the seventh step is to search for possible solutions. Again there are various different techniques that can be used at this stage, and it is advisable to ensure that people have more than one technique in their 'kit bag'. The techniques used at this stage need to encourage both analytical and creative thought. At the creative end of the spectrum, the 'solutions fishbone diagram' is useful and 'force field analysis' is a good analytical tool. Having decided on the best solution based on the facts the eighth step is to present the solution, together with an outline of the method by which it was derived, to management. This is not only the procedure required for communication and authorization but also importantly for recognition of the individual or group whose work is involved. Recognition is an essential ingredient in this whole process and is dealt with in detail in Chapter 20. It must not be forgotten since it is the lifeblood of the whole Excellence process. The solution which is devised should obviously pay due regard to the costs and benefits which will accrue. A key part of the Journey to Excellence is the training of people in the organization to be able to make a business case for the preferred solution. This obviously includes the requirement for calculating at least simple payback periods for investments and to be able to think in the same terms as management, as far as assessing the business cases for any requested expenditure. This should not be taken to mean, however, that the only issues of value which are tackled on the Journey to Excellence are those which cost money and yield money benefits. Many of course will, but there is a whole array of other problems and opportunities which need dealing with in every organization which only indirectly add to the bottom line results of the organization. In these cases, however, it is important that people still pay attention, in an organized way, to measuring the costs and benefits of the actions they propose. Finally, as step nine, it is necessary to remember that the new concept of Quality demands measurement to check conformance to requirements. This final step in the problem-solving structure involves instituting a mechanism for tracking the results of the proposed action. This often will take the form of a simple control chart, but in some circumstances other mechanisms will be needed.

The third major concern when involving people in problem-solving activities is one which applies only to aspects of the Journey to Excellence involving group working. This concern relates to the lack of knowledge and skill which people in general bring to the process of working together in groups. It may seem remarkable but it is certainly the case that most problems which result in groups being ineffective are caused by this, rather than any lack of technical knowledge about the particular subject under review. The whole subject of group dynamics has been, and continues to be, researched both intensively and extensively, and Excellent companies utilize the essence of this work as an organized part of the business of equipping people to be able to play their part in the improvement process and to play it successfully. It is not sufficient merely to teach a problem-solving structure, since any lack of skill in working together will detract from the use of the problem-solving tools. The two go hand in glove, and we need to develop people's skills in both dimensions.

The Journey to Excellence requires that people in the organization work on problems and opportunities in an organized and systematic way and as a part of the process of removing defects from the work which is performed. This does not happen by magic but by people, whether individually or in groups, getting into an appropriate and positive frame of mind, using a sound structure for their work, and, when working in groups, being able to manage the dynamics of the group successfully. Problem-solving and opportunity-seeking activities are key to the achievement of Excellence, and everyone needs to be involved in one way or another. Therefore everyone ultimately needs to be equipped with the knowledge, tools, and skills to play his part successfully. This is fundamental to the process.

Chapter 17

ACTION PHASE 1: 'PUT YOUR OWN HOUSE IN ORDER'

One of the core Quality concepts which must be built into the process is that everyone in the organization must be involved in the process of achieving Excellence. Without this we are quite simply building into our systems permission to have defects. The nature of people's involvement is likely to be different, depending on such factors as the job, the existence of a work group, and the personal preferences of individuals. This is both acceptable and appropriate, as long as the involvement happens in one form or another. This is not of course to say that everyone is likely to become involved simultaneously. This would be unrealistic and unwise, since the mechanisms for involvement require organizing, planning, and supporting in the main. The nature of people's involvement can be as an individual, in groups, or, of course, both. In this chapter we look at the recommended ways of structuring this first phase of the process of getting problem-solving activities going at both a group and an individual level.

Before we begin this it will be advisable to establish some ground rules which it will be necessary to communicate widely at the outset. The first concerns the recognition that the best run companies have problems, as do the best managers. Though obvious, there is a real necessity for us to communicate this message clearly and firmly. The reason is a very practical one. Experience indicates that very often in processes such as the Journey to Excellence there is, at the outset, a tendency for some managers to feel rather defensive about problems and difficulties in their department being revealed and worked on openly, almost in public. This has often led to the strange phenomenon of the 'disappearing problem'. What happens here is that the group which has highlighted the issue and begun to work on it, analyses the issue and then begins to collect data about it. This process of gathering the facts, however, comes to a shuddering halt as the problem disappears, as if by magic, and there are no data left to collect! This is often very frustrating for the group concerned, but in a sense, more importantly, it often indicates that management in the area feel threatened by the potential 'exposure' of their 'dirty washing'. It would not be so bad if the problem had really been solved, but in these circumstances it will usually reappear once the eyes of the world have been diverted onto something new, thus leading to even more frustration for those who had committed themselves to solving it in the first place.

It is of vital importance, if we are to achieve Excellence, that management is not only competent but also confident. The message that is important to transmit is that good managers are always concerned with solving problems and making improvements. In an Excellent company, criticism would not be levelled because problems existed in a department, but it certainly would if there were not mechanisms for working on and solving them. Furthermore, it is vital to promote the message that good managers recognize that they cannot possibly solve all of the problems and exploit all of the opportunities in their department by themselves. Management is primarily about the effective use of resources, and key to the management process is the successful use of the human resource. As such it is the good manager who encourages members of his staff to become involved in activities designed to solve problems in the department, and it is a requirement of the Excellence through Quality process that senior management communicate this clearly to the middle and junior management levels of the organization.

Staff involvement is vital to the process of achieving Excellence, as we have said, and the second ground rule we need to establish is that having staff working on problems and opportunities does not mean that they are doing the manager's job for him. It is everyone's job to use their knowledge and skills to the utmost, in the effort to achieve the stated goals of the organization. It is a very rare individual whose only potential lies in the strength of his arms and legs. We all have brains in our heads and Excellent companies utilize these better than do other organizations. This is not simply a matter of telling people to get on with it, however, since the process needs structure and support. It is the job of management to provide this, and thereby to give people the chance of using their knowledge and skills effectively. The manager's role is not concerned with solving all of the problems himself. Obviously he will work as a problem solver, but a further key part of his job is to develop his staff to the situation where they are both able and willing to become involved, and to join in this whole process on a voluntary and enthusiastic basis.

The third ground rule, which is essential to communicate widely and to work on consistently, so that ultimately it becomes an ethic within the organization, concerns 'doing as you say you will do'. These seven words are amongst the most important of all the thousands that will need to be spoken and written during the Journey to Excellence. All organizations are extremely complex, they require the coordination of many tasks to achieve the appropriate outputs, and many things can go wrong. The real difficulty is that one thing going wrong tends not to remain an isolated incident; it tends to have repercussions throughout the rest of the process, which often leads to the orginal minor problem escalating out of all proportion. Investigation into these occurences in organizations leads to the conclusion that there are things that Excellent companies need to do to manage this effect. Firstly, there is a need to develop in staff a recognition that everyone is responsible for doing what he says he will do. If this becomes an accepted reality, planning becomes easier and more effective, complex action plans will be achieved on schedule, and the whole process of running the business will become more ordered and therefore successful. It is said that NASA was able to put a man on the moon with all the bewildering complexity of that project, mainly because they were able to manage the complexity by everyone doing what they said they would do. It is not a bad proposal that if it worked for them, it is likely to work for us!

A key point about this requirement is that the organization is not asking its staff to break any world records. Unfortunately the impression often gained by employees is that the requirement is for just that. Here we are not calling for anyone to set unrealistic targets, in fact the opposite. It is actually very counterproductive to have people who constantly do this and therefore do not deliver what they say they will. On the contrary, this is a call for sanity in action planning rather than false bravado. Of course we want people to set themselves stretching targets, but achievable ones, and if this can become the norm, a lot of progress will have been made on the Journey to Excellence.

Having established these ground rules it is possible to move on to the steps involved in this phase of the process. The in-department evaluation of activity is the precursor to this stage and will have generated many ideas; it is therefore very important that we organize this process carefully so that momentum is not lost. In practice, the early steps of this phase will almost certainly have been set in motion during the IDEA stage, so careful planning will be required in the particular organization to ensure that the timing is right. It is important to recognize that in an organization of any size the whole process of achieving Excellence through Quality will need to be organized as a series of overlapping phases which are started in different parts of the organization at different times. It will be inevitable, in anything except a very small company, that there will be departments which are a long way down the road before others have started. This should not be a subject of concern; in fact it usually helps in the management and resourcing of the process. Broadly speaking, and as far as possible, the introduction and expansion of the process should be based on the enthusiasm of management in the different areas of the organization. Ultimately everyone will have to join in, but it is better to structure the introduction of the different phases on the basis of interest and willingness, rather than imposition. One of the ongoing tasks of senior management, and also of the Quality staff and steering committee members, is to sell the whole concept over a period of time to those who are sceptical, so that ultimately there is little or no need for compulsion as the process spreads and is introduced in different parts of the organization.

Thus far the IDEA technique has involved departments and sections in defining the tasks that are performed currently. Furthermore, it has prompted the negotiating, agreeing, and measuring of these tasks between suppliers and customers. Finally, it has helped to generate a list of improvement possibilities involving the staff of the individual sections. As has already been said, we need now to deal with both the individual and group activities which encourage people to work on these opportunities. On an individual basis in the long term the primary mechanism for involvement will be via the individual action plans which are generated from the management by objectives and appraisal and counselling systems discussed in Chapter 5 of this book and which progressively need to be spread to cover all members of staff. It is recommended in designing the system that everyone, at least of management and supervisory level, should be a part of a system which involves them regularly in organized discussions with their boss to decide the key result areas for each job holder for the next period of time, usually three, six, or twelve months. Ultimately, as has been said, this system should be extended to include all employees, and where this becomes the case it is further recommended that the time frame of the initial objective setting should be relatively short, say up to three months. The reason for this is that it is important to keep up the pace of the process and to retain a high level of active interest among non-management people. Most people in this situation who have not been programmed via annual reviews, five-year plans, and so on, have a relatively short time perspective, and whereas it will help to work on extending this, in the short term it will be prudent to set goals within it. This process of identifying and setting goals for the key result areas is a general one, and takes in the whole scope of people's jobs. We are using the system in this instance to promote individual responsibility and action specifically related to Quality, and progressively it should be made clear that there should be a specific Quality objective in everyone's action plan at every objective-setting round. Again, caution is required and it is unlikely that it will be wise to impose this on everyone simultaneously from the outset. This is for two reasons. The first is that for people to be able to work on Quality issues effectively they need to have been trained in the Quality problem-solving process and the allied techniques. This is to ensure that staff are able to work on issues in an organized way, and specifically so that they are able to measure their progress and the results of their work. If this is not done it is likely that the whole process will degenerate into a vague, though well-intentioned, drive which will have no real substance to it. The second reason is that if it is imposed on everyone, it is unlikely that there will be a very high level of commitment amongst many, and given this it will take

143

a lot of back-up support, encouragement, pushing, and selling to translate the imposition into any useful output. In the real world such impositions at the beginning are more likely actually to detract from the process rather than add to it.

The practical mechanism which is recommended at the outset for promoting individual activities within the process is called the 'individual quest for Quality'. This encourages and enables people from anywhere within the organization not only to commit themselves to the Quality process but also to begin working on specific issues in an organized and systematic way. It is a voluntary system which is designed to help people become involved even if there are no group-based activities in their area at the moment that they can join. The purpose here is to avoid the potential danger of raising expectations amongst staff and then of failing to meet them. Ultimately everyone in the organization will be required to be involved in one way or another in the Excellence through Quality process, but from the outset it will be better to build the system on a voluntary basis as far as possible since this will breed a higher level of commitment and ownership. An immediate danger, which it is important to avoid when introducing these Excellence through Quality mechanisms, is of people working in a vague, unquantified, however well-intentioned way. It is essential that the basic Quality concepts are both reinforced and promoted through all the activities that go under the Quality banner. As such training will be required for everyone who decides to join this 'individual quest for Quality'. There are systems available to formalize the process, and without wishing to enter into the realms of bureaucracy and red tape, it is important to have an organized mechanism, even if only to be able to provide appropriate recognition for those who choose to take part.

The three core features of such schemes should first be a statement from the individual of his commitment to Quality, which should be formalized in some tangible way. Different organizations use different mechanisms for this, the most common being certificates and mementos of various kinds. The second feature involves an organized statement of the particular commitment being made in this instance. This should involve something within the control of the individual, something capable of being measured, and should include an assessment of the level of improvement being aimed at and the time period involved, together with review dates. Clearly it will assist the credibility of this mechanism if management demonstrate their commitment by joining in. The commitment needs to be recorded in some way, with copies being given to the person's manager and the Quality office, with one being retained by the individual. Initially it should be the job of the Quality office to follow up task activities on the agreed date to ensure that appropriate recognition is given and to encourage new projects to be taken up as appropriate, although this responsibility should progressively be transferred to the line. The third essential ingredient in this system is that those who volunteer to join should be given training in both the Quality problem-solving process and also the simple technique of measurement, control, and tracking, before they commit themselves to the detail of their first project. This will ensure that the targets people set for themselves are realistic and that they have the ability to track their own progress as they make their journey. Where appropriate, these activities should qualify for recognition or suggestion scheme awards.

In some organizations it may be deemed appropriate, after a period of time, to include this process within the standard goal-setting format of the annual review mentioned earlier. This could be decided at the point in time when the annual review is geared up to include formal Quality goals for individuals to work on. Alternatively, in other organizations this mechanism may be retained in its original form, to give continued reinforcement and recognition of people's voluntary contributions to the quest for Excellence through Quality.

As far as group working is concerned the IDEA will have generated many possibilities for action. The IDEA process involves every department in reaching agreement with the people before them in the work process (their suppliers) and also those to whom they pass their work (their customers). Since very many problems in organizations stem from these relationships this very process will always highlight a large area of opportunities for improvement, and what is more, it will promote the general notion of Quality as 'meeting the requirements of our customers now and in the future'.

Of course there is a major potential problem at this stage, which is that most staff know that they have many problems in their interactions with other departments. Furthermore, most people are absolutely convinced that all of the problems are the other parties' fault. This firmly held belief is probably the cause of more frustration and less action than almost anything else in an organization, and needs to be dealt with if the Journey to Excellence is to proceed. Many people will have heard of the adage taken from the often seen 'finger-pointing' posture that, for every finger we point at others, there are three pointing back at us! The belief, however, that 'it is all your fault' is deep, and at the first phase we need to address it specifically by focusing attention on issues that 'we' can deal with. This is why one phase of the Journey to Excellence is called 'putting your own house in order'. It will not be easy, given the extent of this deeply held belief that it is all someone else's fault, to refocus the attention of everyone to the things that they can handle themselves. The processes which are put in place at the time are crucial, not only for the potential that they have in solving problems but also in changing this attitude, since in Excellent companies it is essential that employees have a basic orientation to search for, and work at, the things they can influence themselves. Therefore, at this stage the concentration of the process is geared towards educating people in the need to 'put your own house in order', teaching them how to do it, and providing mechanisms which will enable it to be accomplished.

There are two main group-based activities which are used at this stage of the process, Quality Department Groups and Quality Circles. The IDEA has generated many possibilities for action and it is essential that those ideas are not left to fester. An immediate way that this danger can be avoided is through Quality Department Groups. These groups have been described in Chapter 15 of this book and so at this juncture it is only necessary to describe how they should be set up.

At the outset, however, we should specify an extremely important dimension which should be built into the activities of all Quality groups, the role of facilitator. The facilitator's task in these Quality groups is to help the group work successfully together, not by becoming involved in the technical intricacies of the issue at hand, but by staying out of this and by focusing attention on the way the group is working and the effectiveness of the interactions between members. The facilitator can come from anywhere in the organization and at the outset would be likely to be someone from the Quality staff. It is often an advantage for the facilitator to come from outside the function or department, since if he does not have the technical knowledge to contribute to the task under consideration, there is less likelihood of him being temp-ted to get involved in it and consequently more chance of his focusing on the way the group members are interacting and being able to help in this way, which is his main role. As people in the organization become more knowledgeable and skilled at managing the dynamics of the group, there is progressively less need for a facilitator, but experience indicates that to have someone at hand for each group that is set up is a very necessary and worthwhile investment, whatever the level of sophistication of group members.

The IDEA will have provided a large list of potential subjects for investigation, and at this stage there is a need to prioritize. The first step in working on this will be for management in the department or function to highlight key issues and to formulate Quality Department Groups to tackle them using the Quality problem-solving process outlined in Chapter 16. Quality Department Groups are groups which are 'owned' by management, and as such will focus on problems and opportunities which are seen as priority issues by the management of the particular department or function. In setting up such groups there should be an awareness that many of the issues are likely to be problems which have been present for some time, and some may well have been tackled in different ways at various times in the past. Such issues will benefit from being viewed in a rather different light, and the creative problem-solving process which is used by Quality groups is ideally placed to provide new insights if it is used with skill and care.

At the outset management is faced with the task of selecting prople to take part in these activities. At first glance this might appear to be an entirely straightforward task, unworthy of further comment, but this would be to oversimplify it. In practice the composition of the group is something which can be treated and viewed in a number of different ways. Most people, looking at it in a traditional way, tend, intuit-ively, to look for the individuals with the greatest level of technical competence to tackle the particular subject and will stop there. Whilst this should, theoretically, give us the best solution, it very often does not. There are, potentially, a range of reasons for this. Firstly, it is often the case that technically competent people when working together in groups become so mesmerized by the task on which they are working that they forget, or do not bother to pay much attention to, the way they are tackling it. This often leads to poor group process, characterized by such things as members rigidly arguing for their own solution rather than that which is best for the group, poor listening to the contributions of other members, a lack of willingness to consider different possibilities, and a too rapid closure, often arrived at by the use of conflict-reducing decision-making methods such as voting. Practical experience of groups selected merely for their technical competence leads to the view that they rarely achieve results which do justice to the level of competence of the members, and so perhaps a different approach is needed here.

As far as membership of these groups is concerned, there is often a very good case for including some people who will help to stimulate new and original thought. Such members will often not be amongst those technically most qualified to contribute, and so their inclusion will need to be thought about carefully since they will not 'select themselves' for membership by virtue of their knowledge of the subject. Some people have a particular knack when it comes to creative thinking, and others are able to develop their creative skills by working hard at it. Either way the inclusion of people with creative talent will certainly give these groups more chance of coming up with new and original solutions to old problems if their creative input is allowed to flourish and work, which it should be since the Quality problem-solving process techniques stress the need for such contributions. An element of inquisitiveness and irreverence is often a key ingredient for success, and management should remember this also when setting up Quality Department Groups. One final point on membership of these groups is that though the focus of attention is on 'putting your own house in order', it will often be very useful to include group members from outside the department, since they will often be able to provide useful guidance and feedback. This outsider perspective can often help to overcome the 'insider' problem of 'not seeing the wood for the trees'. It is obviously important, however, if outsiders are invited in, that the conditions surrounding their involvement should be clearly specified. Individual groups will need to define their own expectations of each other, but it is strongly suggested that included in the 'rules' should be firstly that the 'outsiders' are honest in giving their views, whether or not they are positive or negative, and secondly that there should be no immediate rejection allowed by the insiders. Any reaction to negative feedback should be limited to asking questions, for clarification only. The third rule should be that such observations be recorded on flip charts and displayed for the whole group to see, to mull over, and to return to at suitable moments in its work.

In summary, then, the composition of these management-owned Quality Department Groups gives considerable scope for imagination, and used appropriately an element of risk taking can be immensely rewarding in stimulating creative thinking and being able to formulate new solutions to old problems. The Quality Department Groups give departmental management the opportunity to focus on the issues which it sees as being crucial in 'putting your own house in order'.

The Quality process, however, needs to give everyone the chance to participate, not only in solving the problems which management sees as priorities, but on issues which are felt to be important at non-management levels of the organization. The concept which is used to provide this mechanism is Quality Circles. The Quality Circles concept has been described in Chapter 15 of this book and so at this stage we only need to focus attention on the basic stages involved in setting up the Quality Circles part of the Excellence through Quality process.

In practice there are five broad stages that are required for the successful introduction of the Quality Circles. It has already been stated that the concept appears deceptively simple and many organizations have had serious problems and failures with it, through paying insufficient attention to the process of introduction and maintenance.

Stage one in the introduction of Quality Circles is to plan it carefully. The key factors which need to be decided at this point are, firstly, who should coordinate the activity. In most cases this will be the Quality director and the Quality steering group described in Chapter 11. The coordinator role is important in a number of ways primarily to do with the planning of different phases of the introduction and acting as a focal point, not only to solve problems but also to demonstrate commitment to the concept to everyone in the organization. Clearly it will be essential for those in the coordinator role to have a good understanding of the concept, and ensuring this is an activity which is tackled at this time.

Of course there should be no doubt, having come this far on the Journey to Excellence, of the genuine commitment of top management, but it will always be as well to check back on this. Quality Circles represents a part of this overall management philosophy and is an essential ingredient which must be introduced at some stage, but it does require commitment to a genuinely participative style of management, as well as to the time and the costs involved in setting up and maintaining the Quality Circles groups. Furthermore, it is a long-term commitment that is required and so it is essential to clarify unequivocally that the requisite level of support is both understood and given.

The next task at the preliminary stage is to decide on some of the practicalities of the initial launch. Firstly, we need to have an idea of how many groups we wish to start up during phase one. The clear rule of thumb with Quality Circles is to start small and grow big. It is very unwise, even in the largest of locations, to start up with more than six or so groups, and even this level of launch will require a full time resource, or its equivalent, to set up and support to an appropriate level. In smaller locations fewer groups can be started, though it is always unwise to begin with just one group, since this not only puts all of the eggs in one basket but also puts a lot of unwarranted pressure on the leader and members of the group to be successful.

The second aspect of this practical planning stage is to ensure that there are suitable places for the groups to hold their meetings. Simply to push the Quality Circles into a corner of the canteen will quickly be interpreted by members as an indication of the real level of commitment to the importance of these activities. More Quality Circles groups than one would like to mention have stopped meeting for precisely this reason, so it is an issue worthy of careful thought and planning. Another dimension of the same issue concerns the situation which happens all too often where the Quality Circle's meeting is pushed out of its planned meeting room because another 'more important' management meeting needs the room. It happens, and it always leads to the same inevitable result.

Training is an essential ingredient in the successful introduction and maintenance of a Quality Circles programme, and training material is required. As such there is a need to research the training packages which are available on the subject and to decide whether or not to use one of these, or to invest in producing customized material within the company. Either will be perfectly acceptable given that it is done well. It should be said, however, that developing professional training material is an expensive business and most organizations choose the option of purchasing a generalized package and then adding to it as required by the particular nuances of their organization. There is no doubt that to introduce Quality Circles successfully requires both knowledge and skill, and so as well as training material the organization needs to consider the extent to which it may wish to use experienced outside consultants to assist in the early stages of the introduction. The final task at this stage is to establish who will provide the facilitator back-up to the groups. The facilitator role, as has already been said earlier in this chapter is vital to all of the group activities which play their part in the Journey to Excellence, and no more so than with Quality Circles. The particular role of the facilitator with these groups becomes clear when it is realized that the members, and often the leaders, tend to have relatively little experience at working in problem-solving groups—indeed at group working of any sort. As such there is a need for particular skill, care, patience, and tact when helping, especially in the early stages. Most usually facilitator training programmes will be conducted to furnish the organization with appropriately skilled people in both the Quality problem-solving process and also the main considerations which are important in group working if the activities are to be successful. In large organizations these courses will be held regularly so that there is no shortage of either part or full time assistance in getting Quality activities off the ground. As has been said before, it is important, wherever possible, that full time facilitators are used, but in the real world it is likely that they will need to be supplemented by part timers who focus on one or two groups.

The second stage of introducing Quality Circles involves holding briefing meetings for management, supervisors and unions and introduce the concept in detail. These briefing meetings are best organized as relatively small groups of up to about twenty people, and should be geared to outlining the concept of Quality Circles, as described in Chapter 15, and to briefing people on the plan of introduction of the concept into the organization. There is also, at this stage, the requirement for letting staff know what is happening, since the concept represents a major opportunity for their playing a part in the Excellence through Quality process. Clearly at this early stage there is a danger of raising expectations too high too quickly, especially when we consider that the concept will be launched on a small scale at first. Staff should be introduced to the general concept and plan of introduction, usually via a brochure or simply a briefing sheet. It should be made clear in this that though ultimately everyone will be given the chance to join in, it is vital that the groups recieve sufficient back-up and support and that therefore this will take some time to organize. Everyone will, however, have the opportunity to participate in the overall process from the outset through the 'individual quest for Quality' system which is described earlier in this chapter.

As a part of the briefing meetings held with supervisors, there should be a request for any first level supervisor who is interested in being trained as a Quality Circle leader to put forward his name. At this stage it is best not to call for volunteers to start Circles, since supervisors will be in a better position to decide after the leader training programme. The first leader course, which usually lasts for three days, should train more leaders than the number of Circles it is planned to start, so that people can genuinely feel free not to begin if they do not want to. At all stages of this process it is very important that management up the line from those who volunteer are kept informed, and that their active support and encouragement is sought. If anyone is against the participation of his supervisor it will be best to delay in that area, and spend time trying to convince and convert that manager before going ahead, since in the long run his active support will be essential if the concept is to be introduced and maintained successfully.

The third stage involves running the initial Quality Circle leader training programme for the volunteer supervisors. This can be done either by using external consultants or internal resources and gives the opportunities for potential leaders to practise the problem-solving techniques which form the Quality process, to learn about the mechanisms of running a Quality Circle, and also to begin the process of developing a fruitful relationship with the facilitator. Quality Circle leader courses generally tend to be of three days duration. It is essential that this part of the process is not skipped, since there is a much greater likelihood of Quality Circle groups failing if they are being run by untrained leaders. At the end of the course the participants should be invited to volunteer to start up groups in their working areas, and the group as a whole should be involved in making any decisions about this.

Given the decision about which leaders will offer Quality Circles to their people, the next step is to run introductory briefing meetings for staff in the relevant sections and to invite volunteers to come forward from amongst staff. Given that the volunteers are forthcoming, as they always are, the fourth stage involves starting up the groups in the relevant areas and helping them to become successful. Quality Circle member training is always best conducted during the course of tackling their first problem, and is best arranged on a 'need to know' basis. Thus the techniques are not seen as theoretical but as practical tools for tackling real world problems. The role of the facilitator during this stage is vital, and the relationship between him and the leader is the really important one. The task of the facilitator is primarily to help the leader and group to become self-sufficient, and this should be in the forefront of the minds of those undertaking the role. The process could well take six months or longer, and is not a race, but the underlying goal is to achieve self-sufficiency in the operation of the group, based on well-trained, well-developed, and highly motivated leaders and members. During this stage it is also essential that the managers in the heirarchy directly above the Quality Circles be kept in touch and aware of the workings of the group, and that their commitment and encouragement be sought constantly, not only in private, but overtly and directly to Quality Circle members and leaders.

The final stage of the process of introducing the concept is to build on the successes of the first Quality Circle groups by communicating these effectively and using them to encourage more people to want to start. After the first few groups the expansion of the programme can develop fairly rapidly, but it is absolutely essential, firstly, that it be done within the core principles of the approach and, secondly, that the expansion is resourced appropriately, especially with the requisite level of facilitator back-up and support to all of the groups. It is all too easy to forget these in the anxiety to expand, and often it is a critical time as groups struggle to get themselves up and running again after their initial success. There can often be a feeling of having 'fulfilled the purpose' or of anti-climax, after their first presentation, and it is obviously vital that the groups are encouraged to continue and build on their early success by selecting a further problem or opportunity to work on.

This phase of the Journey to Excellence is ongoing. The basic tools and techniques which the individuals and groups require to ensure that their work leads them further down the road towards Quality and defect-free performance are taught at this stage. Clearly during this phase there is a considerable investment of time required to train and educate employees in the understanding and use of the Quality problem-solving structure. It is an essential prerequisite to their involvement in Quality-based activities, and it is therefore utterly essential that it is done and done well. Different members of staff will, of course, be trained in different ways and at different times. Some will learn the techniques through their involvement in Quality Circles, others in Quality Department Groups. Some of the techniques will be learned by individuals through the 'individual quest for Quality' programme.

People working in departments and sections will always have 'a house to keep in order', and as such their Quality Circles should simply become part of the way they do things. Equally managers will often need, and want, to use Quality Department Groups to tackle important issues as they arise. Individuals need to be able to work on Quality issues either in groups or by themselves in an organized way, and whether it is via the 'individual quest for Quality', the management by objectives system, Quality Circles, or Quality Department Groups, there is a permanent requirement for organized mechanisms to help structure the effort and help people to ensure their success.

Chapter 18

ACTION PHASE 2: 'THE BITS BETWEEN THE BOXES'

Phase two of the Journey to Excellence takes on board the recognition that although companies tend to be organized functionally and hierarchically, work tends to take place across functional boundaries and departments. To give a simple example, an order is received in the sales department, passed to production for manufacture, the product is sent to the warehouse for storage and then distribution, while the paperwork is sent to accounts for billing. The work process, then, is not the same as the organization structure on the heirarchy, for they form the skeleton and are there to organize and control the people in the organization. Work processes on the other hand are the bloodstream; they represent the way that useful work gets done, which leads the organization to the achievement of its objectives. A work process is a series of actions or decisions which flow in a sequence and lead to a specified end result. The normal 'rules' of Quality need to apply to these series of activities, in other words that each one should have measurable and measured inputs from suppliers and outputs to customers. Furthermore, since the process represents the way the organization uses its resources to achieve its goals, the process itself is repeated at whatever frequency is appropriate. We can represent this visually as shown in Figure 1.

The main processes of any organization will almost invariably cut across functional boundaries, and this will usually be the case even when the main processes are broken down into subprocesses, for the purpose of detailed analysis. There are occasions, however, when this is not the case, and there is no intrinsic necessity for them to be cross functional. A further important point relates to the role of individual tasks and decisions, and is the recognition that a single task can play a part in more than one work process.

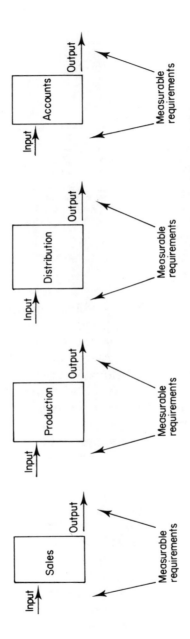

Figure 1. A Work Process

154

There is much that can be done to achieve Excellence by 'putting our own house in order', of this there is no doubt. Equally there are many problems, issues, and opportunities that can be, and all too often are, overlooked if this is the sole focus. It is often staggering to find the extent of the simplification of work processes which is possible when they are looked at in an organized way. Jobs become embedded within processes which at the time seemed, and maybe even were, logical and useful, but for whatever reasons are not now needed for the fulfilment of the requirements of the next customer who receives the output. Most organizational processes are capable of really substantial improvement, simply because most people's time in organizations is spent devoted to heirarchical and functional issues, and very little has hitherto been spent looking at the process by which work gets done. The fundamental purpose of this phase of the Journey to Excellence, then, is to look deeply into these processes, to simplify them wherever possible, to ensure that they are efficient and effective in meeting the needs of the customers in the process, and to leave in place tracking systems which will signal the continued meeting of requirements, or sound an alarm if the process begins to throw up defects for whatever reasons.

The first requirement if this is to be achieved will, of course, be to decide what the processes of any organization are. This is not an easy task, for altogether there are likely to be hundreds of them in an organization of any size, if we include all of the subprocesses under the main headings. There is no pre-prepared list of processes which apply to all organizations, so the job of defining them has to be undertaken afresh in each case. This may seem at first to be a little awe-inspiring, but there is no real requirement for a full and complete analysis to be made from the start; indeed this could be counterproductive, since it is unlikely that it would be possible to work on such an amount of information all at once. As with most of the steps on the Journey to Excellence it is much better to take them one by one and to 'make haste slowly', typically by working in one department after another or with one process after another, rather than attempting to deal with the whole organization simultaneously. At the outset, however, it will be important for the senior managment group to meet, with a view to determining what the main overall processes are within this particular organization and appointing those who will be responsible for these processes.

Firstly, the decision is made about what are the processes. A process has a beginning, a variable amount of 'middle', and an end. As such the definition of a process should start with the clause, 'This process begins when ....' It should continue to define the main stages which are included in the process, in verb/noun statements, and should conclude with the clause, 'This process ends when ....' The definition of the process does not go into the minute details of each task, merely the broad steps. It is a little dangerous to give examples of work processes which different organizations have defined, since it may lead people to assume that there are predetermined answers, which there are not. At the macroorganizational level, however, the processes will be broader and likely to be a little more generalized than the subprocesses further down the line, so it is possible, and maybe useful, to give examples. Typical processes at this organization-wide level could include things like procurement, distribution, billing, accounts receiveable, and personnel. To take one of them, the definition used in one organization to define its billing process is, 'The billing process begins with the receipt of information, which can come from a wide range of sources and which triggers the calculation of the correct amount, the updating of customer record cards, and the creation of an invoice. The process ends with the reporting of results to financial accounts.'

Having got this far, the next step is to appoint an 'owner' for each process. Normally in organizations, managers 'own' parts of the heirarchy, a section, department, or function, but nobody owns the process of work. This omission is a major reason why there is invariably so much scope for improvement in this stage of the Journey. Ultimately every single process and subprocess must be owned by a specific single manager. It is a job which should always be a high priority in the job objectives of the person concerned, and is something which cannot be delegated. It is also an ongoing responsibility since it involves not only improving or simplifying the process as an initial activity, but instituting tracking mechanisms and constantly updating it to ensure that it adapts flexibly to the changing requirements of the customers who receive its output, and the business as a whole. The decision as to who should be owner of the various processes and subprocesses can be made in a variety of ways, but should basically attempt to share the responsibilities among those who have real and practical interests in the particular area being covered. It is obviously important that it is managers who are appointed, or who volunteer, for these jobs, since a considerable degree of executive authority will be needed to ensure that the appropriate actions are indeed taken in both the analysis and the implementation of improvements. One person can, of course, be the owner of more than one process or subprocess.

One of the initial tasks of the main process owner will be to establish how he wishes to tackle the task. Most people in this situation choose to bring together a small group of those involved in different aspects of the overall process, which is then broken down into the relevant subprocesses. Doing this and allocating owners of these subprocesses then gives a 'natural' group which can be responsible for the work that needs to be done, and has the added advantage that it helps the overall process owner keep track of what is being done to improve the subprocesses.

The responsibilities of the owners of the processes and subprocesses can be viewed under three main headings, the first of which is to understand the process. This is by no means as easy as might be expected, since processes are virtually never mapped out in the way that organization structures are, and are often very complicated, but nonetheless it is a key requirement. The second responsibility is to establish the mechanism for analysing and managing the process without, of course, undermining the normal functional executive process. This requires skill, tact, and sensitivity if we are not to leave people, especially managers, feeling threatened. One of the main reasons that process management is phase two of the overall journey, following the focus of phase one on 'putting our own house in order', is that during phase one employees are trained not only in problem-solving skills but also into a state of mind which is positive, confident, and opportunity-seeking rather than defensive, geared to finger pointing, and aimed at maintenance of the status quo. As such they are equipped to be able to handle the different demands made by phase two, with its focus on cross-functional issues, specifically that individual sections do not feel the urge to defend the status quo, at least in their part of the process. The third responsibility of the process owner is actually to ensure that the process is efficient and effective and also adaptable to meet changing circumstances. Furthermore, the owner should ensure that key measures are taken to track progress and are reported regularly.

Having defined the process and designated the owner, it is necessary to provide a mechanism for investigating the process and highlighting opportunities for improvement. Two possibilities are proposed, one simpler and easier to arrange, but less detailed and therefore less accurate. There are occasions when each technique will be of use. The simpler one is called process perceptions analysis (PPA). This involves six steps, the first of which is to arrange a meeting between the managers of the different parts of a process to agree that there is a mutual willingness and commitment to analysing and working on simplifications and other improvements. The task can appear daunting. It requires time, and sometimes a considerable amount of time, so there needs to be a willingness to pay this price. On the other hand, the task can be accomplished over a period of time, since the analytical tools recommended tend to break down into convenient stages, so the time and energy devoted to the job can be spread out so as not to disrupt the normal work of the departments involved. Another relevant point about the use of the word 'willingness' is that it is neither realistic nor sensible to think in terms of simultaneously working on all the business processes. We would be better served by identifying enthusiasts and working with them at the outset, since it will often be the good results of the first few activities which will serve to sell the idea to others and therefore encourage its spread, on the basis of the active desire of managers within the processes to become involved, rather than the imposed demands of the organization to do so. Ultimately, of course, everyone will have to join in, but in most organizations it will take a long time to get to the point where compulsion is required.

The second step is to hold a meeting of the managers/supervisors who are involved in the process or subprocess which is under scrutiny. The purpose of this meeting is to determine whether all of the broad stages of the process, or indeed the process itself, are in fact necessary. Tackling this question requires people to be able to think openly and creatively. If we only use the conventional logic of the day, the answer will always be that everything is necessary and important, whereas looking at things through different eyes often changes the picture. In one major organization a department of twenty-five people was responsible for checking expense claims, correcting them where appropriate, and recycling them back to line management for approval. This was the way things had always been done, and the department worked very efficiently at its task. Very little simplification of the process was possible because it had been refined over the years. The group of managers responsible for looking at the subprocess of expenses claims during this second stage of the PPA realized, however, that this whole part of the process was, actually, unnecessary and that the responsibility for this series of tasks really rested with line management. They retrained managers, provided a comprehensive briefing document and various other aids, and were able to close down the expenses checking department. The staff concerned were then utilized doing work which was really useful and also more interesting.

The key to this stage is to encourage managers to take off their blinkers and really to question the usefulness of the present system. Because this is easier to say than to do it is often appropriate to have a third party run the meeting. In general a half or full day will be needed, depending on the complexity of the process. Before the meeting the process owner will have defined its broad stages and recorded them in as simple a format as possible. This work will often be accomplished with the help of a facilitator or, in the early days, a consultant. At the meeting itself it will be necessary to get people to take off their blinkers and think creatively. This, of course, requires more than simply saying the words, and the third party should be prepared for an appropriate amount of input, training, and practice to encourage those involved really to break down the barriers which tend to inhibit creative thought in most of us. The structure of this meeting should be firstly to consider what could happen if each part of the process or the whole of it were done away with. Following this, if the answer is anything other than that it can be removed, the next question should be 'so what?' This forces the group to consider again whether the activity is really vital.

Stage three applies to the parts of the process that are perceived to be really necessary to the accomplishment of the goals of the organization in an effective way. It involves arranging meetings between people at adjacent parts of the process, in other words a meeting for every customer and supplier relationship. This will often involve two separate groups, but sometimes will involve individuals when only one person performs a task before passing it on. If large groups of people are engaged in the same work it will usually be appropriate to select a representative group to undertake the task rather than to involve everyone. Both of the managers or supervisors of the particular sections or departments must be at the meetings, and need to play an active part. The meeting needs to begin with an agreement between all involved to be constructively candid, not to point fingers, not to be defensive, and to solve any problems on the basis of the facts rather than opinions. The next step is to send the two groups, or individuals, away with a brief to create a number of lists, as follows:

1. The things we believe we do well
2. The things we believe we could improve on
3. The things we believe 'they' do well
4. The things we believe 'they' could improve on
5. The things we believe 'they' have got on their lists
6. The things which we believe we could stop doing
7. The things which we believe 'they' could stop doing

This part of the process having been completed, the next step, stage four, is to share the lists, at this point without discussion apart from any clarification that may be necessary to ensure understanding. It may in some cases be sensible to continue with stage four at a subsequent meeting, but this will depend on circumstances.

Step five involves a discussion about improvement opportunities. This should be organized to ensure that, although the meeting is conducted in an orderly fashion, those involved feel free to think creatively and explore hitherto unforseen possibilities. The first question to be tackled should relate to parts 6 and 7 of the list, concerning opportunities for cutting out tasks which have become redundant or could be achieved in a more effective way by someone else. All the notable points in the discussion should be recorded on flip charts as the debate is progressing, not just any recommendations or decisions, and this procedure should be continued for all the remaining steps. The meeting should progress naturally, at appropriate points to a comparison of the other lists. What often happens here is that people are more critical of themselves than are the other party. This can lead to very useful and positive results as far as improvements in communication, morale, and mutual respect are concerned, although there is somewhat of a danger here that the two parties begin to form a mutual admiration society which accepts the status quo and ceases to search for improvements. The manager, facilitator, or consultant running the session obviously needs to be on the lookout for this, and should try to keep the meeting focused on active possibilities, within the loose structure provided by the two sets of lists. Action points should be summarized into those which are clearly necessary and should be proposed for immediate introduction and those where a trial period is needed to test the idea. This stage should include the formulation of action proposals for presentation to management, with an analysis of the estimated benefits of the suggestion in both tangible and intangible terms.

In the event of two groups failing to agree on an important issue during this whole process, it should be agreed at the outset that a Quality Task Force would be set up containing nominees from both groups and a facilitator, with the express purpose of collecting the facts pertaining to the area of disagreement and then reporting those facts back to the two full groups. Since the groups have committed themselves to the use of facts rather than opinions this should assist the resolution of such issues, although often it will also require the skilled assistance of the facilitator or outside consultant.

Having highlighted the possibilities for improvement either by increased efficiency, simplification, or ceasing to perform the task, and having presented the idea to management and received any necessary approval, the sixth step involves setting up the appropriate activities to ensure that the ideas are fully investigated and used. Many of these groups will be QITs, building on the enthusiasm of those involved to make sure that improvements are made. Other issues may be highlighted by the process which management wish to pursue. This is, of course, an entirely legitimate outcome of the technique, and in this case a Quality Task Force might be established to achieve action on the issue concerned.

Process perception analysis is a simple and unbureaucratic mechanism for seeking improvements in cross-functional processes. As has been seen, it involves staff in searching out possibilities within a structure. A key part of the process, however, is the initial meeting at management level to establish whether or not the activities are necessary at all. Staff usually cannot be expected to answer such a question since they will not usually have access to enough information to get a picture of the whole situation. Because the technique does not plot the process in great detail it is possible, even likely, that opportunities may be missed. Nonetheless, it represents a tool which can stimulate significant improvements and it has the advantage that it is less time consuming, more involving, and simpler to understand than most of the alternatives, and can yield an added benefit in increasing the confidence of staff in being able to deal with or improve complex cross-functional processes. It is of particular value, in some circumstances, as a first pass through the maze of process management.

The second technique for use at this stage is a method for analysing processes (MAP). Although the format of the technique and the questions asked are few and simple, the whole is an immensely powerful mechanism for looking into the intricate detail of work processes with a view to highlighting opportunities for simplification. The technique involves line management specifically and requires the use of a trained internal practitioner or consultant. Whereas the PPA technique often generates a high level of ownership of the improvement process amongst people at the task level, MAP tends to be owned more by management. Staff are involved in a series of structured interviews to get at the core detail of their activities, but it is, generally speaking, a management activity to use the results which emerge from the analysis. There are six stages which make up this procedure, the first two of which are the same as the initial steps in the PPA described earlier. There are countless examples in organizations of tasks which are being performed very efficiently, but which actually are not necessary and can be scrapped. As such there is a need to look at the overall process and the broad steps which make it up, with a view to trying to establish how essential is the work and what would be the consequences of simply not doing it at all. This, as was stated before, requires that people think creatively and that they are not hidebound and afflicted with tunnel vision. This is not easy to achieve since most adults do tend to be very boxed in by precedence, in other words by the way things always have been done, and often find it difficult to take off their blinkers. For these reasons it is as well to build in some training in creative thinking as a part of stage two of the MAP.

Step three of the process involves briefing, and then interviewing, members of staff who are engaged in the tasks which make up the process. Where a number of people are engaged in performing the same task there is no need to interview everyone. The interviews themselves should be performed by a trained facilitator or an outside consultant. The purpose at this point is to establish a detailed picture of the tasks which are performed and which make up the process under review. We are interested in what is done, when it is done, how often, and a range of other aspects which will enable us to position the tasks within the process, understand the various dependencies that there are between tasks, and evaluate the opportunities for improvement. This is a not altogether easy thing to do, and requires a thought-through format which will make it easy to draw conclusions from the analysis, or at least not make it overcomplicated.

In practice the interviews are exploratory sessions based around three basic questions. The first question asks what the job holder actually does when performing the particular task under discussion. The answers should be expressed as statements of activities. This question is followed by an exploration of how long it takes to do the task and how often the tasks are performed. The second set of questions looks at any other inputs and help that are received whilst performing the task, and explores who gives those inputs or help, how much help is given, and how it is organized. This gives information to build up a picture of the linkages and dependencies which surround the task. The final question asks what the job holder does after having completed the task, which gives the information necessary to trace the process onto its next step. Having held these structure interviews, the next step is to document the process in a way which is easy to work with. This will usually involve constructing a flow chart since this seems to give the clearest result.

Step five involves management meeting together to consider the process as a whole now that it has been specified in detail. The purpose here is to consider the process itself, rather than the individual tasks which make it up, and to ask whether any of the component parts of the process can simply be done away with. This, of course, has also been done at stage two, but not on the basis of the detailed analysis which is now available. This step will, again, require a lot of open-minded and creative thinking to perform well, and the 'devil's advocate' role will be a key one in exploring the possibilities really thoroughly. Liberal use of 'what if' questions will be important here, as will the response, 'so what?', to avoid possibilities being closed off too quickly.

The next question to be explored during this phase is whether it will be possible to simplify part of the process, or indeed the process in its entirety. This might involve dramatic change, for example with the recognition of an opportunity for automation, or alternatively a chance to organize the way things are done currently in a new, simpler, and better way. The next question asks whether it would be better, even if all of the tasks are necessary, to perform them in a different order. Anything that remains, having withstood the scrutiny, can be assumed to be a necessary part of the process.

Step six widens the search for improvement opportunities by arranging meetings between managers and job holders, within their individual sections and departments, either as individuals or, if more than one person performs the same task, groups of job holders. These meetings focus on three questions and encourage people to think of hitherto unthought of possibilities. Firstly, those involved, including the manager or supervisor, are encouraged to think of whether the task can be simplified in any way, by missing out parts of it, whilst still ensuring that it is performed to standard. Secondly, from the job holder's perspective, can it be changed in any other ways to good effect? This might involve either changing the component parts of the task, changing a working method, changing the order in which the job is done, or changing its positioning within the process. Although this has already been considered in the previous stage, it is eminently possible that the performers of the tasks think of new possibilities which should not be missed out. The third question to be employed here assumes that the task is necessary and that it has been simplified and changed where possible, and asks what can be done to improve the efficiency with which it is done in an effort to serve the recipient of the work, the customer, better and with a higher liklihood of providing the product, component, or the service right first time, or defect free. This last step in many cases would be best handled through the Quality Circle, if one exists, in the particular department or section.

The MAP technique in some ways sounds more complex than it is. It plays an utterly essential part in the Journey to Excellence, however, and it is vital that it is properly understood. Therefore to facilitate understanding it may be useful to include a short and simple example of how it works and can help to identify improvement opportunities. The example comes from a production environment, but of course the technique is applicable to any work process. The subprocess in the example was defined as 'production information', and concerned the flow of information relating to production issues within a major manufacturing facility. The example relates to three tasks, the first of which was the responsibility of the production clerks and was defined as 'to collect the production figures from the production department'. This task involved the following activities:

Collect the previous day's production figures from each line daily and before 9.00 a.m.
Enter the figures onto the production summary pro-forma.
Give the pro-forma to the management accounts clerk when he/she comes to collect it.
The second task was the job of the management accounts clerk and was defined

as 'to fill in and circulate the production report form'. This was analysed into the following activities:

Collect the production summary pro-formas from the production departments before 9.00 a.m.

Collate the figures onto the master production sheet.

Calculate totals, yields, and performance against target.

Photocopy.

Take completed sheets round to the production departments before lunchtime.

The third task was again the responsibility of the production clerks and was described as 'to enter the production figures on the master charts'. The activities in the case were described as:

Receive the master production sheet from the management accounts clerk.

Enter the relevant output figures, yields, and performance against target, onto the master control chart in the production manager's office.

Photocopy the master production sheets.

Circulate to supervisors and section heads.

This way of doing things had persisted for years in this organization and was considered quite simply 'the way it's always been done'. The MAP technique enabled those involved in this work, which took a total of eight hours of time each day, to reorganize the process to the extent that today it only takes four hours to produce the same output. This result was achieved during stages five and six which were outlined above. At stage five, management recognized that it was not necessary for the management accounts clerk physically to go round the production units—this was a legacy of the past when systems of communication were less effective. It was easier to telephone, and this saved two hours. This group furthermore recognized the potential problem of the initial tasks of both the production clerks and the management accounts clerk being required to be finished by 9.00 a.m. The possible problem was that the management accounts clerk could be left waiting for figures to be made available. On checking it was confirmed that this was the norm rather than the exception, and so the timings were altered to allow an overlap and thereby ensure that there was no waiting. This saved a further one hour per day.

During stage six of the process the members of staff involved in the management accounts Quality Circle identified an opportunity for further gains in efficiency by producing a set of calculating tables for yields and performance against target figures, which saved them a further hour a day. The result of this part of the MAP, for this particular part of a subprocess, was an improvement in terms of time expended of

50 per cent. It is, of course, a humble example, deliberately so to aid communication. Others have saved millions.

PPA and MAP are two immensely powerful mechanisms when they are used with skill and care. They address an aspect of the organization which is rarely tackled in any orderly fashion, that of the work process. That it is rarely tackled accounts for the fact that so many issues and problems in organizations are ones that have 'fallen down the cracks' or, in our terminology, relate to 'the bits between the boxes' of the organization chart.

Techniques PPA and MAP are designed to help optimize processes. A key to understanding this stage of the overall process of Excellence through Quality is to recognize that circumstances change. As such it is essential to realize that the process owner's job is an ongoing one. Furthermore, it needs to be recognized that, when they are introduced, processes need to be capable of adapting to changed circumstances. The Journey to Excellence is a journey rather than a destination, and the effective management of work processes is fundamental on this journey. It should be recognized, however, that work processes are also journeys rather than destinations, and therefore that management of the work processes is a process in itself. The success attained in working on achieving continuous improvements in these processes as times and circumstances change is the process of becoming and being Excellent.

The ultimate objective of this whole stage is that the organization can be wholly confident that all of the work processes employed are entirely in order and operating without defects. This of course will not happen simply because we hope that it will, it requires a massive and consistent effort to make it the day to day reality of the organization. Since most organizations have so far to go on this journey, it is sensible to have some milestones to guide us on our way. Having said this, we do not want a 'rating' system which is so unwieldy and bureaucratic that it deflects time and energy away from making progress on the journey itself, but it will be useful to have a mechanism for giving feedback, motivating, and keeping track of where we are across the range of processes in the organization. A simple and staged marking system is recommended, which should be administered by the Quality department in collaboration with the relevant process owners. Within reason it does not matter how many points there are on the scale. More than about seven tends to increase bureaucracy and involves people in fine distinctions which are not entirely the purpose. Equally to have just three points on the scale tends not to give enough scope for differentiating between processes which are genuinely at different stages of their development. Somewhere between four and seven points on the scale is right in most circumstances. A six-point scale could involve the following steps:

1. *The beginning.* No process owners have been agreed, no active consideration is being given to managing work processes.
2. *Getting started.* Process owners have been appointed, have held initial meetings,

and have established subprocess owners who have also held initial meetings.

3. *Making progress*. Processes have been analysed in an organized way and improvement activities have begun at the individual and group level.

4. *Big steps*. Major improvements have been made to simplify, reroute, or abandon processes or subprocesses which are not needed. The processes are beginning to be controlled and monitored on a regular basis.

5. *Stabilizing*. Process management is a part of normal business. All processes and subprocesses are being tracked as a part of the normal routine and largely by those involved. The search for improvements is a continual quest, and one which everyone plays a part in and enjoys. The focus here is not only on problems, most of which have been solved, but on finding ways of making things even better than they are. Groups are able to form and disband as appropriate to deal with problems that arise and are well equipped with the skills required to make a contribution.

6. *Sophistication*. Processes are defect-free, effective, and efficient, and are measured routinely by those involved. The search for improvement goes on in the light of changing circumstances external to the process, and it is these which keep people on their toes and continue to tax their abilities. The processes are not only efficient and effective, but highly adaptable to changing requirements.

Such a system needs, of course, to be kept in perspective, but especially it should be taken seriously. There is no point in having it if we treat it flippantly or manipulate the results. Its purpose, as with all the tools and techniques used on the journey, is to assist the improvement process. 'The journey of a thousand miles starts with one step' and no one expects full-scale process management to be in place at the start of the journey. What the organization which embarks on the journey will expect is that progress is made, steadily, towards the ultimate destination. As such, the simple tracking system proposed is designed to give feedback to those concerned and to enable them to measure their progress. It is not a club with which to beat people. If it is treated as such it will lead to manipulation of 'scores' to avoid being 'beaten over the head', and this whole phase of the journey is simply too important for this to happen. All work processes should be the subject of a regular audit to track progress, and this is a responsibility of the process owner in collaboration with the Quality director. External assistance is often valuable in doing this, not only to achieve an unbiased view but also since sometimes looking in from the outside can assist in seeing things more clearly for what they really are. It will obviously take a long time, years in fact, to get to a stage where all business processes have reached the stage of sophistication outlined above. Achieving this, however, is the cutting edge of Excellence, but do not be tempted to rush into this stage too quickly at the expense of previous stages. The cutting edge of any knife will not be improved by honing it on a soft, crumbling, or irregular stone. Excellence is achieved by managing work processes effectively, but on the basis of a culture within which all employees recognize their role as suppliers, their responsibility for providing defect-free work, and their skill to achieve these things. The day to day practice of the organization will be to 'put our own house in order' and maintain it that way, within the framework of a viable and responsive set of basic business procedures and on the bedrock of a clearly defined and disseminated core mission and organizational philosophy.

Part 5

MAINTAINING INTEREST—
THE SALESMEN

Chapter 19

MARKETING THE PROCESS

The word 'marketing' conjures up for many people a vision of young and rather trendy people who seem to spend a lot of time at lunch! More serious than this is the almost universal perception that marketing is solely concerned with the external image of the goods and services sold by the organization, and with the ongoing attempt to encourage customers to choose our offerings rather than those of the competition. Clearly the marketing departments of organizations as presently constituted are charged with this work, but for us to make progress on our Journey to Excellence we need to add a new and vital dimension to the word.

To put it simply, we need an internal marketing programme that sells the ideas and concepts of Excellence through Quality within the organization to all of our employees, and does so in as professional a way as is done with our external marketing. We should say immediately that this new dimension will not necessarily be the job of the marketing department, though it would seem senseless not to tap their experience and knowledge. In practice the responsibility falls on the shoulders of the Quality director, at least to coordinate the activities. The process of marketing goods and services to actual and potential end users is never ending, as is testified by the countless stream of advertisements which bombard us from hoardings, magazines, and on television, radio, and the cinema, and the same can be said of the internal requirement which supports the Journey to Excellence. We should not feel in any way different as far as this is concerned. For most organizations, clearly, it will be a radical and maybe rather strange concept at first. We have, however, in Excellence through Quality, a superb product to market, and we should give it all the support that it deserves.

The marketing strategy which is devised for the Excellence through Quality process should be developed just as if we were dealing with the end products or services of the organization, and this involves understanding the two different dimensions of the marketing process. The first aspect aims at creating an awareness of the product and the development of a positive basic attitude amongst potential customers to what we are marketing. This aspect is often called 'theme' marketing. Consider some examples. An oil company puts a series of advertisements on television which show beautiful views of the countryside, with wild animals prospering in their natural habitat. The camera zooms over wide tracts of these idyllic surroundings. The purpose which lies behind all of this is to explain that these views are of the countryside after the organization in question has laid an oil pipeline. What has this got to do with the forecourt of the local fuel station? Not a lot at first glance, and that was not the idea. The purpose was to create an ambience, a feeling that the company in question was trustworthy, public spirited, and had a highly developed social and ecological conscience. Which of us would not feel happy about buying their products after this kind of exposure?

One of the giant automobile companies decides that their need is different. They are concerned about the way that their market has been assailed by the seemingly unstoppable Japanese invasion. They know, because of the market research they have done, that one of the main reasons for this concerns the quality of the Japanese offerings. Their strategy does not only involve television, it also includes every brochure, hoarding advertisement, and every car. The message is simple and focuses on the fact that Quality is 'the number one job' in the company—a few simple and well-chosen words which people will see time and time again. The hope is that the message will be accepted, almost subliminally, until quality and the manufacturer's name are synonymous. The marketing people in this example are not trying to sell any one type of car, but rather the whole range and the whole company.

A fast-food chain is concerned about its image with the public, and wants to let people know how warm and friendly it is as an organization. Again the strategy is different. The first thing that needs changing are the colours that it paints the shops, for blue is such a cold colour. A lot of money is spent researching the colours which go with food and which also promote a warm and friendly image, and even more is spent on redecorating the sites. This is all backed up by advertising on radio, television, and the hoardings which assures us of the really friendly welcome we will receive when we go to any of the chain's restaurants. Again the result of all this money and effort is not to make us rush into the first of the company's places we see; it is meant to soften up our attitudes rather than immediately to stimulate our appetites.

As far as our Journey to Excellence is concerned we also need to work on people's attitudes in the same way that the marketing in these three examples has done, but before we can do that in any precise way, we need to be sure that we know what the word attitude means and what are its constituent parts. An attitude, simply stated, is a predisposition to act, and in the examples stated above there was a very clear desire to develop a predisposition amongst potential customers to act in a certain way.

It is also essential if our marketing is to be successful for us to know what attitudes are made up of; basically they are made up of two parts. Firstly, an attitude consists of all the things we know and have experience of in relation to the particular issue. Clearly we have attitudes about a whole range of things—drugs, work, the relative merits of baseball and cricket, almost everything we come into contact with either directly or through the media—and what we know about the issue forms the so-called cognitive part of our attitude. The second part of our attitudes are all the things that we feel about the subject in question. So our attitude towards our children consists of everything we know and have experience of concerning them, and also everything we feel about them. Equally our attitude to football is made up of our knowledge and experience on the one hand and feeling about it on the other.

All other things being equal it is most likely that our behaviour will fall in line with our attitudes. If we have had good experiences of a product and feel comfortable with it we will tend to continue buying it. What we are trying to do with this aspect of the internal marketing process, then, is to generate in all employees a positive knowledge and experience relating to the Journey to Excellence and also positive feelings about it all, so that having sampled the product they will want to keep 'buying' it for ever.

The theme marketing we undertake in-company is unlikely, however, to use all of the same mechanisms that have been discussed so far, for example pure television advertising internally within an organization is unlikely to be appropriate in the majority of cases. Clearly there is a wide scope for creativity in designing the marketing strategy, and it would be unwise to be too prescriptive about the requirement in this book, though it will be appropriate to pass on some ideas and experience from organizations which are already engaged on the Journey to Excellence. Theme marketing focuses on putting a message in front of people and keeping it there, making sure that no one forgets it.

As far as we are concerned there are two main key messages that are required to be put across in the early months, and maybe even years, of the process, the first and maybe most important of which concerns the unfailing commitment of top management. New ideas, which are often introduced as permanent 'life saving' mechanisms, seem frequently not to stand the test of time in organizations. Because of this most people seem now almost to assume that changes which are introduced will be one or other form of short-term gimmickry. Top management commitment is called on, given, and then forgotten so often that in many places it is treated almost as a joke. It is absolutely essential that we avoid these traps on this Journey, but it will require a lot of good marketing to achieve it. The first golden rule about this piece of the campaign, then, is that the commitment of the top has to be given, and given explicitly and specifically. Furthermore, it has to be given for precise business-related reasons, rather than as something which would be rather nice to do. Everyone in the organization must get this message, and must have it reinforced in different ways over an extended period of time. As such it will be appropriate to think in terms of having different vehicles for getting over the message, including such things as videos, company or department meetings, letters to all staff, noticeboard announcements, tannoy announcements, articles in company newspapers, and so on, as well as day to day discussions with whoever is in earshot! The message should be couched in different ways for the different mechanisms, to keep it from losing its edge, but it is often a good idea to have some kind of slogan or symbol which remains constant to give people something standard to relate to and to reinforce the basic theme.

The second requirement of the theme campaign is to publicize the philosophy and core mission of the business with a view to ensuring ultimately that all members of staff not only know what they are but 'live' them in their everyday working lives. Again there are different ways of doing this and there is no need to rely entirely on any one. Prominent displays of these statements are usually a good idea, not only on noticeboards but also in meeting rooms, offices, and on the production floor. They are statements which are designed to guide and help employees in their day to day work and so need to be around where the work is being performed. Whatever the mechanism used, the words, of course, will remain the same, since ideally every member of staff should be able to repeat the statements verbatim and understand what they mean in a practical, real-world sense.

The second dimension of our marketing strategy is rather different. It is commonly called 'scheme' marketing. The oil company referred to earlier does not only want people to feel good about the company in a general way, it wants to get people into its garages buying its petrol. What is needed here is some interest and excitement to attach to what is basically a rather dull product. There are many options, and in this they do not want to be limited or bogged down. They decide that a free glass offer with 10 gallons of fuel for a three-month period will do the trick. This is followed by a 'win a million' promotion involving scratch cards. We never seem to go past the filling stations without some new gimmicky scheme being advertised.

The car manufacturer decides that, to get people actually buying one particular model that is not doing too well in terms of sales, they will reduce the price by offering a guaranteed trade-in price for our old car or a straight reduction on the list price. To add power to the campaign, they offer free credit for any car bought within the next month. A few months later they move on to a different idea—a free radio and cassette player with every car bought between now and Christmas.

The fast-food chain is worried by the competition cutting prices and so responds in kind by reducing the price of hamburgers for two weeks. Wanting to attract and retain the child market, it negotiates an arrangement to give away ET Tee-shirts with vouchers received each time a meal is bought. A little later, wanting to promote a new chicken concoction, it arranges sampling sessions and gives away a piece of the chicken with every two cheeseburgers bought 'for a limited period only'!

We are all aware of this kind of marketing. We are constantly bombarded by advertisements which offer us the chance to win dream villas, free groceries for a year, new cars, and myriad other things. There seems to be a limitless supply of ideas to keep up the day to day interest in the goods and services on sale, and we need to use our own creativity to make sure that the same is the case with our own internal marketing campaign. Again this is not a subject about which to be prescriptive, but there is no harm in sharing some of the ideas that have worked for different organizations. Since many of the activities which will lead us down the road to Excellence are based on group problem-solving, many companies have pens and folders printed with their slogan and give them away to group members. As with many of these devices, the payback in terms of interest and a feeling of recognition always far outweighs the costs involved. Some companies give away high-quality leather binders and expensive pens to members of groups for recording their notes and claim that such give-aways are easily paid for in the benefits. Badges, tie pins, brooches, and so on, inscribed with the logo the company has designed to symbolize the Journey, are again common ideas. Writing pads or blotting pads, pre-printed with Quality messages or the company philosophy, have been used very effectively by many, certificates work in a range of organizations, and diaries are good value since they last a year! With all of these ideas the decision is needed as to what the rules will be that govern the give-away. Sometimes it is appropriate to have a free distribution to everyone, whilst on other occasions there is more meaning, and therefore effect, if it is linked to something, whether this be membership of a group or the solution of a problem, for example.

Give-aways are one aspect of scheme marketing for internal processes such as this, but they are not the only one. Poster campaigns can be very useful in keeping interest at a high level. These can be based on posters which are available commercially, but there are other more imaginative possibilities as well. Many organizations encourage artistic members of staff to create their own posters for display whilst others invite suitable quotations from staff to emphasize a particular aspect of Excellence through Quality; these are then illustrated appropriately for display around the organization. With poster advertising, and indeed any such public display, including noticeboards, it is important to ring the changes fairly frequently, so as not to let the messages become stale. It is not so much that familiarity will breed contempt, rather that if the same poster is left in one place for a long time, people will stop 'seeing' it—it will become just part of the furniture. It is better to keep them moving around.

Another type of activity which can help to add interest involves organizing visits either from or to other organizations that are involved in a similar way on the Journey to Excellence. Such exchanges can not only give ideas, but stimulate and motivate everyone who takes part in them. 'Open days' are one example of this kind of activity, as are various kinds of seminar or conference. Some organizations run their own, others prefer to visit, but the purpose is the same.

The marketing strategy for the Journey to Excellence requires both theme and scheme elements. It needs to be thought through carefully and imaginatively since it plays an important role in sustaining interest and keeping up commitment, and clearly the activities which go to make up the campaign should be of the highest quality in themselves. Since the marketing requirement is an ongoing one, it will be necessary to keep track of any changing requirements that there are to fulfil the need to sustain pace and interest, and this may involve engaging in some simple internal market research to pitch the activities at the right level. The whole process of achieving Excellence should be an enjoyable one for everyone in the organization, and appropriate marketing can facilitate this.

Chapter 20

RECOGNITION

In study after study conducted by organizations and by independent academics about the motivations of people at work, the word 'recognition' comes out as amongst the most important and powerful. In informal studies among managers concerning the perceived motivation of subordinates, the words 'money' and 'working conditions' dominate the conversation. The gap in perceptions is alarming and the consequences are even more so. As far as the Journey to Excellence is concerned it is of absolute importance that adequate recognition is built in to the day to day behaviour of the organization, since this is the fuel which will keep many people motivated on the road. It is a subject worthy of serious thought, even though there are no truly universal rules about it, except that organized mechanisms for ensuring that enough recognition is given must be in place from the start. This point is worth reinforcing. Many organizations leave the planning of such aspects until there appears to be a need for them. By doing this recognition is all too often relegated to the status of something which is 'nice' to do rather than its rightful position as something which we 'need' to do as a priority item. Furthermore, because, generally speaking, the pace of the process increases, the reality is that people who deserve formal recognition during the early stages sometimes miss out. Even worse, because there is always so much to do in getting the process off the ground and working successfully, some companies have omitted to do anything about this vital subject and have thus built in the seeds of destruction for their Quality movements.

Recognition is something for which, in a perfect world, we would probably be able to depend on being entirely spontaneous, but of course this is not a perfect world. As such, most organizations really do not think about the way they wish to handle this vital requirement. There are many different ways of organizing recognition programmes and there are probably some cultural differences which will be reflected in the mechanisms which are put in place. The most common types of recognition are dealt with in the next few paragraphs, and although experience indicates that it is unwise to make too many predictions about what would be acceptable in any culture or environment, since there are undeniably cultural differences, it is often surprising how many things are acceptable and how ideas which might have been assumed to be inappropriate are in fact welcomed by employees. Therefore it is sensible to go through at least the main ideas that organizations all over the world use as a basis for handling the issue of recognition.

The role of money is perhaps the appropriate one to begin with since it is always, and quite rightly, a subject for discussion. The first point which is important to raise is that money is not the only useful form of recognition, neither is it necessary at all in many cases. There are many recorded instances of people and groups, notably Quality Circles, who have solved problems and done work which has qualified them for monetary awards under suggestion programmes of various sorts, and who have rejected such awards or, more often, declined to apply for them. When asked why, the most common response has been that they 'were not in it for the money' or that 'getting money for this work would spoil it'. Many people have expressed amazement and disbelief that something of this kind could happen, and even more say that though it might happen elsewhere, there is no way it could possibly happen in their organization; yet it can and it does. The reason why this phenomenon does occur is that people from the lower echelons are, frankly, not used to receiving any form of recognition from the organization, so when it does happen, at least for the first few times, there is often a reaction which is designed not to 'contaminate' the recognition with the normal currency of work, in other words wages or money. Interestingly employees in Excellent companies are much happier about sharing the proceeds of their work, because recognition is a fundamental part of the philosophy of the organization and accepting money does not demean anyone or undermine the motivation which lies behind the effort. People in these situations will not worry that their colleagues and the organization will assume that they only did it for the money; indeed they will be confident that there is an understanding that people who choose to become involved in working towards Excellence want to be a part of the journey— and furthermore that sharing the benefits is a natural dimension of it.

None of this is meant to imply that money should not be used, just that its role should not be taken out of proportion. Before moving on to other forms of recognition it is important that we clarify what it is that we should be recognizing and rewarding, and again the role of money looms large. In all too many cases the only thing that is recognized is the value of the savings made by individuals or groups. There are a number of problems with this which are worth reviewing. Firstly, there is a danger, if only money savings are recognized, that the voluntary types of group, Quality Circles or Quality Improvement Teams, feel that the only valued contributions are those which generate tangible benefits. This has the effect that the real feeling of ownership of the group begins to be undermined and the commitment wanes in line with the realization that the ability to select their own problems is really a rather hollow charade. In practice these groups can contribute a wide range of very useful work which really does assist on the Journey to Excellence but which does not always generate directly attributable tangible benefits. Ultimately any worthwhile problem solving will represent another step on the journey, and it is important that groups and individuals get the message from the organization that such issues are worthy of people's time and commitment to solve.

A second problem is that if management assumes that the organization only recognizes money savings, it is highly likely that they will put pressure on individuals and groups only to tackle issues which are likely to yield such benefits. This will certainly undermine the ownership of these activities and reduce them to the level of 'management-owned' techniques or, worse, management manipulations, which they are not of course designed to be. In such circumstances the voluntary groups and individual activities will quickly fade out usually leaving a rather disappointed and frustrated set of employees in their wake. A further problem here is that in such circumstances there will be a vast array of problems and opportunities that are missed. Organizations that have kept detailed records of the work done, notably by Quality Circle type groups, have found that about a quarter of the problems tackled yield a directly attributable financial benefit which is solely and unequivocally due to the work of the Quality Circle. A further quarter of the issues tackled yield a concrete benefit, but not solely due to the work of the Quality Circle. The remainder of the problems and opportunities are not capable of being quantified in terms of money in any really useful or meaningful way. The great majority of these issues are, however, significant, and represent a useful contribution on the Journey to Excellence. The evidence which emerges from a wide range of organizations of all types and sizes, and from all industries, indicates very clearly that the groups which do save money sometimes do so in a big way, and that the overall results of such activities contribute significantly in money terms to the performance of the business. If the process is encouraged along the pure guidelines indicated, this will happen. Equally, experience indicates also that if management focuses on and chases too hard after the concrete benefits, it undermines the whole process very quickly.

The key in all this is the realization that the process is more important than the result. It is really the use of an organized problem-solving structure, tools and techniques for analysing problems, gathering and interpreting data which should be recognized, along with the enthusiasm and commitment of the particular individual or group. If it only ever seems to be the groups which save vast amounts of money that receive awards or are invited to make presentations, staff will quickly get the message and will become disheartened and frustrated when they cannot think of a revolutionary idea that will save a great sum of money. Staff in general want to contribute in a tangible way, and this is why they join these groups and activities. Management needs to recognize good contributions, which will be measured in some way because Quality is all about measurement, but regardless of whether or not the benefit can be usefully expressed in terms of money. It is always beneficial, especially in larger organizations, to have guidelines to assist in this, so that groups can be confident of being recognized according to the same set of criteria. The guidelines set out below are those used by IBM's Endicott location in New York State and are reproduced with their permission.

Recommended criteria for team circle recognition

Effort and attitude (weight approximately 30 per cent)

Membership	—	(participation, self-development, improved problem-solving ability)
Operations	—	(leadership, cooperation, training)
Meetings	—	(preparation, scheduling, documentation)
Follow-up	—	(complete assignment, tracking in place)

Technique and procedure (weight approximately 30 per cent)

Objective selection	—	(relevant to team/circle, relevant to organization, clearly understood and documented)
Action plans	—	(practical, well understood, well implemented)
Discussion/investigation	—	(problems well understood, date complete and correct, proper evaluation, thorough discussion by team/circle)
Checking	—	(consistency with accepted practices, tracking appropriate)
Reports	—	(well organized and complete, on time, well presented)

Accomplishment of objective (weight approximately 30 per cent)

Problem solved	—	(base cause identified and corrected, re-occurrence prevented)
Analysis complete	—	(data evaluated, measures and tracking evaluated)
Solution optimum/practical	—	(best potential solution chosen, implementation achievable and reasonable)

Implementation effective   —   (directly attacks problem, shows improvement in reasonable time/effort)

Follow-up measurement   —   (tracking system in place, periodic review in place)

Value of accomplishment (weight approximately 10 per cent)

Value assessment   —   (direct elimination of inefficient use of time, resource, dollars)

Bonus weighting of 10 per cent should be considered where solution demonstrates exeptional originality or inventiveness.

There are two key points that emerge from this which we can usefully draw on and learn from. The first is that in these guidelines money benefits only count for 10 per cent of the overall 'marks' awarded, and in practice these tangible benefits do not have to be expressed in money; they can be calculated in other way, such as the use of time or other resources.

The second key point is that quite clearly and positively it is the process of problem solving which is being reinforced and rewarded, not in any vague, general and global way, but specifically and precisely through the defined criteria.

Having established these as ground rules we can now move on to discuss the types of recognition which are appropriate on the Journey to Excellence. In a speech recently a senior executive from a major corporation stated that in Japan the highest form of recognition was to be allowed to give a presentation to the chief executive, and that people and groups vie and compete with each other to be allowed this singular honour. He contrasted this to the West where giving a presentation to the chief execu- tive usually equated with trouble, and was to be avoided like the plague! In practice the recognition process in many companies offers the chance to make a presentation to the top managers as the ultimate accolade, and it seems to work just as well as a mechanism as it does in Japan. The story gives a warning that it is often a mistake to assume too much about cultural differences. This is not to say that there are none, for clearly there are, just that they are often less serious than might at first be imagined. There are really five broad categories of recognition and organizations will probably choose to use a combination in structuring their approach.

The first category is universally acceptable and includes what might be called the permanent or semi-permanent mementos. The most commonly used of these are items such as folders and binders and good quality pens suitably printed with the Excellence through Quality logo and possibly the participant's name. Where such things are used it is obviously important that they are of a suitable quality themselves if they are to have a positive effect. These items are generally used as recognition for volunteering to participate in the 'individual quest for Quality', Quality Circles, or Quality Improvement Teams, or for having worked through and solved a problem via one of these mechanisms. They should not be given away to people other than those who qualify, since this only serves to undermine the basic value of the 'award' to those who have genuinely earned it. This is easy to say, yet remarkably difficult to do, since these mementos usually acquire a considerable perceived value; however, it is an important point.

The second type of recognition which is very commonly used and accepted is the awarding of certificates. Though ridiculed by some people, notably some of those with higher academic qualifications, this is an important mechanism and should not be overlooked. This is so especially in relation to group activities, though in many circumstances it should also be used for individual work. Certificates obviously need to be of high quality, they need to be framed, and they must be signed on behalf of the company by a suitably senior person. Often large organizations have a range of certificates to reflect different levels of recognition.

The third type of recognition includes the award of such things as breakfasts, lunches, dinners, theatre tickets, and so on, for the employee and his or her partner. These are clearly going to be more expensive than the awards mentioned in the first two categories, and this is in line with the idea of there being opportunities to recognize groups and individuals for exceptional contributions 'above and beyond the call of duty'. Furthermore, such awards have an important place in organizations that wish to reflect different levels of recognition as a part of their programme. In situations such as this it is important to recognize that such awards should be part of a ladder if they are to be used effectively. Every activity should have to start at the bottom rung in these situations and work its way up on merit, in accordance to the rules or guidelines governing the process in the particular organization. If this is not the case there will always be potential problems of elitism and favouritism which will detract from the very real motivational value of such awards.

Fourthly, management presentations, conferences, and other events where groups of employees are able to explain their solutions to problems to their senior managers are a universal and vital mechanism. The importance of two-way communication has been stressed in Chapter 6 of this book, and this method of recognition is also a way of promoting it. There are a wide range of ways of assessing such mechanisms for recognition. Internally, especially in larger organizations, there is the opportunity of structuring a ladder of presentation opportunities. Thus a group may be invited to present their work on a number of occasions, to progressively more senior audiences and with progressively more valuable additional recognition. Ultimately such opportunities to present the work can lead groups to the chance for acclaim outside their organization, through the various mechanisms which exist to promote such activities. There are associations, notably for Quality Circles groups, which are already in existence in most countries and these can provide a useful focus, as can locally organized user or interest groups. Perhaps the most important aspect of this level of recognition, however, is that which is internal, and although competition is good and healthy in some ways, it should wherever possible be structured to allow all groups which achieve the criteria to receive the recognition. In other words, a pure 'win/lose' competition should be avoided in these events since it can end up with people feeling that they are 'losers' rather than 'winners'. This would be tragic since, of course, everyone in this situation is demonstrably a winner. This does not mean that organizations should always avoid the 'Japanese style' competitions to decide which Quality Circles should receive the ultimate accolade of presenting their work at a public convention, since on the way to the honour, groups will have received other progressively greater expressions of recognition. Indeed if it is culturally acceptable, such forms of recognition are extremely powerful and important.

The fifth form of recognition is money. Many organizations already have mechanisms for encouraging and rewarding ideas amongst employees. Usually called suggestions schemes, these mechanisms are primarily designed for the individual. Often they fizzle out after an initial blaze of interest and excitement, mainly because they are not put within any meaningful context, such as the Journey to Excellence. It is not that people are either devoid of ideas or that they lack the motivation to put these forward, merely that, out of context, such mechanisms make little real sense to the average employee and certainly do not actively motivate people to use their undoubted talent in thinking of new and useful possibilities. Where there is a suggestion scheme already in place it may be decided to allow Quality teams access to the rewards allowed under it. In such situations it is important that the guidelines surrounding this are established at the outset, since suggestion schemes are almost universally phrased and organized to promote and reward individual rather than group effort. Furthermore, they focus on rewarding people for ideas outside the normal day to day job requirements of the person proposing the ideas. They are aimed at what could be termed the 'bathtub ideas'! With the voluntary Quality teams, such as Quality Circles, the whole idea is that they 'put their own house in order'. As such the solutions that they devise will be directly concerned with their day to day departmental activities. There is a need to carefully think of how to amalgamate such ideas into existing programmes. It can and has been done, but it needs careful thought, and some companies have decided that it will be better to set up a Quality award scheme which is designed to include group work and suggestions from within the normal job responsibilities of the employees. If it is decided to do this it is obviously important that a win/lose situation is not set up between such a scheme and the existing suggestion programme.

A final level of recognition, which really forms part of the internal marketing process, includes potentially a whole array of 'gimmicky' ideas which are designed to be fun, to breathe life into the process, to keep it visible, and to give people the chance visibly to commit themselves to it. We are talking here about such things as stickers, tie pins, hats, tee shirts, indeed a whole array of possible promotional mechanisms. They are designed to be fun, and they should be fun. Do not worry that the items or ideas here are short lived and disposable, for they are there to create impact. Many of the ideas and items here will be minor, even trivial. This is not a worry since there is a need for 'scheme' marketing as described earlier. At the more serious end of this form of recognition are a range of possibilities for people at all levels to commit themselves publicly to the Journey to Excellence. These will usually take the form of some kind of individually or jointly signed statements by managers and staff stating these commitments. These statements would typically be framed and displayed for all to see, rather like pictures of our families that we have on our desks or at our workplace.

Recognition is an essential ingredient on the Journey to Excellence and it is also an ingredient which can and should be fun. Achieving Excellence is very rewarding as far as the organization is concerned, and these rewards need to be shared; therefore serious and creative thought needs to be given to formulating the mechanisms for doing this in a way which suits the particular organization. Clearly the formulae will be different, and this is all to the good; the key is that any organization wishing to achieve Excellence needs to recognize the contributions of its employees in a generous way, a public way, and a meaningful way, for without them Excellence will not be achieved.